I0029232

THE NATURE OF CHOICE IN

CASEWORK PROCESS

The Nature of Choice in Casework Process

by

Anita J. Faatz

Introduction by VIRGINIA P. ROBINSON

THE UNIVERSITY OF NORTH CAROLINA PRESS

Chapel Hill

Copyright, 1953, by
The University of North Carolina Press

MANUFACTURED IN THE UNITED STATES OF AMERICA
BY THE WILLIAM BYRD PRESS, INC.
RICHMOND, VIRGINIA

PREFACE

I T HAS BEEN my purpose in this book to examine choice in motion; that is to say, choice as it occurs in actual experience, especially the way in which choice unfolds dynamically in that particular instance of experience that we know as the functional helping process. Inevitably there appear in these pages questions of philosophical and ethical import, timeless in nature and fundamental for the understanding of any life process: questions having to do with change and permanence, emotion and reason, freedom and necessity, self and other. But here these questions are tested out in reality, explored to find those attitudes toward the one who seeks help that seem most effectively to foster the development of the capacity to change, to grow, to choose.

As I come to the conclusion of the task which I set myself, I am struck by the realization of how inexhaustible the subject is, how rich in promise for further exploration. I have had to give up the assumption that the capacity to choose is innate and natural to the self, on behalf of the acknowledgment that the mature capacity to choose is earned through growth. And I have, at times reluctantly, relinquished the passionate devotion to the ideal that freedom of choice must be guarded against all encroachment, in order to understand that the quality of inner freedom is rare and always only partially known, but once possessed needs no defending in the usual sense of that word. Its very vulnerability comprises its life.

Those conversant with contemporary psychological and psychoanalytic theory will recognize the sources of my point of view in the psychology of Dr. Otto Rank. It was not my privilege to know Dr. Rank during his lifetime, since my connection with the Pennsylvania School of Social Work (in any substantial way) began in 1940, a year after his death. At times I have felt a great loss in not having known him as a helper or as a teacher, and I have envied those to whom this was an actuality.

Yet I have been advantaged in that I have had simultaneously the unusual experience of being helped in a truly functional process, toward the goal of becoming a teacher, at the same time that I discovered in Rank's writing the exact and precise illumination of the moment in which I lived. To put it in his own words, "for once experience and pure psychological understanding are simultaneous." I would not for one instant presume to voice an opinion on Rank's place in the history of human experience and thought, yet I would be leaving incomplete my acknowledgment to him were I to leave unexpressed my belief in his greatness, and my conviction beyond doubt that he understood in ways that go to the heart of the life process.

Similarly, my gratitude to Dr. Jessie Taft, and especially to Miss Virginia P. Robinson, lies deep beyond the reach of words, and I am content to have it so. One thing only would I like to say, that the peculiar quality of my gratitude derives from their teaching: that only at last in becoming responsible for one's self does true freedom lie.

I should like to express my thanks for many experiences that have been imbued with life, which reach far back to my early strivings as a social worker. To the Maryland Department of Public Welfare with which I was associated for so many years—to its Director, Mr. J. Milton Patterson, and to my friend, the Assistant to the Director, Miss Elizabeth G. Smith—I wish to express my appreciation for the unmistakable evidence that service under public auspices can be sustained on levels of genuine helpfulness and responsibility. I know full well that what I have written here regarding casework may not carry self-evident proof that casework is appropriate in the public social services. But my own interest in choice began in public assistance, and I hope that those who are concerned with this question of the suitability of case-work process for social work in government will find here further opportunity to test out their questions and arrive at their own judgments in the matter.

Finally, I wish to express my grateful appreciation to the School of Social Work of the University of Pennsylvania for the opportunity to pursue my doctoral studies, of which this book is the outcome, and for the privilege of the lively, stimulating experience which is the reward to one who works with agencies, supervisors, and students in this training process.

Philadelphia, Pa.
November, 1952

CONTENTS

PAGE

Preface   v

Introduction by Virginia P. Robinson   xi

PART I

CONTINUITY AND CHANGE: A DEVELOPMENTAL
VIEW OF EMERGING CASEWORK PROCESS

   I   Aspects of Process in the Development of a Profes-
       sion   3
  II   The Special Qualities of the Individual Unit   9
 III   The Search for the Therapeutic Factor   19
  IV   The Discovery of Function   34

PART II

CHOICE IN CASEWORK PROCESS

   V   Statement of the Problem: The Ultimate Single
       Nature of Choice   47
  VI   The Client's Initial Movement Toward the Social
       Agency   55
 VII   The Quality of the Caseworker's Identification   63
VIII   The Will to Help   77
  IX   The Meaning of Acceptance in the Caseworker's
       Response   86
   X   The Nature of Understanding in Casework Help   95
  XI   The Significance of the Immediate Present   103
 XII   The Relation of Content to Psychological Change 110
XIII   The Movement of the Self in Choice   127
       Notes   138

INTRODUCTION

THE PUBLICATION of a new book in the field of social case-work, whose literature is limited for the most part to the conference paper, the short article, or brief pamphlet, is an event of significance for this professional field. I am honored by the invitation of the University of North Carolina Press, its publisher, to introduce this book. For myself, in my position of professor emeritus on the faculty of the University of Pennsylvania School of Social Work where I have been in active teaching and administrative positions for many years, I welcome this opportunity to express to social workers and to the North Carolina Press my appreciation of the continuity which this volume establishes for the theory and practice of the functional point of view in social casework.

The title which Miss Faatz has chosen for this book is immediately challenging and suggestive, not only to the professional caseworker but to every human being who approaches the problem of living and choosing in the world today with curiosity as to the nature of his own choices and concern for the continuity and integrity of the self that makes those choices. The title of Part I, "Continuity and Change," and the chapters which develop it, express a sense of continuity underlying change and development that is rare in this young professional field whose definition is still in the making. The "search for the therapeutic factor" in casework process, the beginnings of which were heralded in the publication by the North Carolina Press in 1930 of my book, *A Changing Psychology in Social Casework,* has been carried by Miss Faatz through two decades of development with a clear and undeviating sense of direction. That this historical evaluation can be affirmed by the two people whose names are most closely associated with this search and with the discovery of function is evidence of the accuracy

with which Miss Faatz has absorbed and appraised the past
as she carries it into the present.

But the more important contribution of this book lies not
in the historical background of Part I but in the dynamic
and original description of process in Part II. The debt to
Rank's contribution to psychological understanding of inner
experience and relationship process is acknowledged fully
and precisely by Miss Faatz in her Preface, but the process
she describes grows immediately and authentically out of
her own experience in the helping processes of casework, of
supervision, of teaching, and administration. Her point of
view has true individuality at the same time that it comprehends and expresses universal meaning.

Miss Faatz has limited her discussion to the helping processes of social casework not only because it is in this practice
that her experience and her competence lie but even more
because of the singular importance which the problem of
choice has assumed in this field. As she sees it, the conflict
between freedom of choice and external compulsion constitutes the basic dilemma in which this helping profession is
entangled, determining differences and conflicts in practice
as well as in theoretical opinions. To my knowledge this
problem has never been grappled with so fundamentally as
in this volume. The psychological solution to which this
analysis points, "the ultimate single nature of choice," must
be read in full and cannot be summarized. Only those individuals who are willing to go beneath the surface of con-
ventional attitudes and externally determined choices to examine the long slow process of internal choosing will read
this book to the end. Those who lend themselves to reading
in this way will find this book deeply rewarding not only
for an understanding of social casework practice but for
finer understanding of helping processes in any profession
or of any life experience in which the problem of the relationship between self and other has become conscious.

                                   VIRGINIA P. ROBINSON

P A R T   I

CONTINUITY AND CHANGE: A DEVELOPMENTAL VIEW OF EMERGING CASEWORK PROCESS

. . . The organism which lives is a thing that endures. Its past, in its entirety, is prolonged into its present, and abides there, actual and acting.

HENRI BERGSON

.

CHAPTER I

ASPECTS OF PROCESS IN THE DEVELOPMENT OF A PROFESSION

IN UNDERTAKING to present a comprehensive view of case-work process at this time, a special problem arises, and a very interesting one, out of a consideration of past, present, and future, so far as casework practice is concerned. The problem is one of assessing accurately where we now stand, for a purpose related wholly to the on-going movement. Social phenomena in their growth processes, like the growth process of the individual, reflect developmental phases, now highly accelerated, now slowing to a halt; now gathering substance upon a plateau; now backward, now caught in immobility; and now again suddenly illuminated by the swift shock of momentary understanding. To articulate the known is to possess it more fully. To possess it more fully is to gather in and consolidate the substance and strength of what is, in order that it can be given more generously to the evolution of what can be.

Whereas the title of this book suggests a partial considera-tion of casework process—that part which I have called the nature of choice in this process—it is in fact a consideration of the whole in a very particular sense. The nature of choice constitutes a central focus at the core of the subject which operates to hold the detail in constant relation to a central idea, so that no outer boundary or limitation is necessary. No case material has been utilized, and in consequence the reader must supply his own illustration. No particular field of casework practice has been held in mind. This discussion is in every sense of the word an exploration of the common base which underlies all casework helping; it does not develop in any detail the specific differences in particular casework services, important as these differences are. Simultaneously there is a common and universal base in which all helping process rests and there is a distinguishable and fine and precise difference in each function which operates with crucial importance in the helping process.

One aspect of this problem of assessing where we are today arises on account of the clear indication that the field of casework practice is comprised of two distinct and opposite points of view,[1] and when this is acknowledged, it becomes equally clear that few if any generalizations will apply to the whole of casework. What is described here is the professional practice now solidly established with distinction and precision as the functional method of helping. The differences existing in point of view in the casework field today are dealt with only on occasion as illuminating contrast, especially in Part I dealing with the development of functional practice, where it is just this divergence which clarifies the two opposite directions in which casework thought and practice have moved.

Another aspect of this problem of assessing the situation today originates from the discouragement which caseworkers often feel on account of the attitude of the public in relation to casework practice, an attitude which at times seems hardly to know that such a thing as casework exists; or, when it does become aware of this fact, is often impelled to attack because of the change and difference which social work represents. It is natural enough that the caseworker's whole relation to the field should be colored by the fact that casework is seldom if ever wholeheartedly wanted by other professions, and that the effort to establish itself as a profession has been an uphill climb. But caseworkers are coming to realize more and more that this is but an inevitable phase of reaction to difference, to change, to fear of what the psychological represents. This is nothing to despair of, so long as the prominence of the problem does not obscure the reality of the remarkable, phenomenal growth in casework practice which has in fact taken place. For the first thing which might be said about casework at the present time is that the development, especially during the past twenty years, has been swift and substantial both in extension of casework method to new services, and particularly in breadth and depth of psychological concept and understanding of a skill which can be taught and learned in responsible process.

Roughly speaking, the term casework has been in use for some fifty years as a means of designating a method of helping which takes place between individual helper and one seeking help. Immediately, when one uses the words individual helper, the necessity arises to add the further observation that this helping takes place always in a social agency setting, as representative of an agency. But at this point this added fact obscures the meaning, in that here we are considering only the one single isolated fact that casework is a process between two individuals, in contrast to other social work processes which concern themselves with numbers of people and with economic and social programs of various sorts. In this respect, namely, that casework is devoted to the one, to the importance of the single, separate life expression, there can be no difference of opinion.

At times, however, there has been a great dissatisfaction with the lack of precise definition for the term casework, and efforts continue in many quarters to force into the mold of logical and watertight definition that which defies every attempt to define. This pressure toward definition has at times been a very compelling one. Its origin is both inner and outer: inner in the sense that it reflects the conflict of the individual caseworker who, trying to help but baffled and unsuccessful in his efforts, projects this discomfort upon the profession in terms of a conceptual drive to define and to prove in absolutes. In turn, this projected pressure becomes a group phenomenon, so that the profession as a whole has at times turned against itself this fierce attack to force a kind of definition and a kind of proof which its longing for sureness seeks in the external world.

It marks a singular advance both in the profession and in the individual helper, that this compelling pressure to define has at last given way to the greater strength of a wholly different kind of precision. There is a kind of definition which is organic, which holds its unity and identity through a central core of concept and reality, which admits its complexity and its life movement, and does violence to neither by force of the human intellect. To some who are oriented within the older natural science philosophy, with its reliance upon precise definition and proof, and its veneration of reason and logic to the exclusion of emotion, the inability on the part of casework to lend itself to precise definition is viewed as evidence of flaw and failure, requiring some day to be corrected if casework is to reach its scientific stature. But to others this capitulation to the intrinsic nature of casework reflects an acknowledgment that casework belongs with that philosophical movement in human experience which seeks new ways to comprehend the dynamics of living, and at last acknowledges the inescapable fact that life will not yield its meaning to him who would attempt to force it into the rigid mold of causal determinism. Wherever the life process has been genuinely understood, this result has come about through a deep devotion to the effort to understand the way it is: imbued with change as well as permanence, tinged by the irrational as powerfully as by the rational, given meaning by emotion, heightened by fear and guilt and evil as truly as by its opposites, and always, in its swift flight in time, defying the effort to arrest its movement or hold it in the hand. Within the helping person who is genuinely related to this process there lies at bottom this deep capitulation to, and admission of, the limitation to understanding; but precisely on this account, paradoxically, new understanding is the reward.

That casework can be described in terms of what it does, the kinds of problems with which it deals, the setting of the social agency in which it is located, the characteristics of the clients who come, goes without saying. It can also be communicated in psychological principle and concept, and its process can be known in ways far more reliable than words alone afford. The nature of growth within the helping person which the casework skill demands can be known and communicated provided always that the reader brings to this task a willingness to seek within his own experience for the understanding which the written word can only suggest; and provided too there is readiness to yield some measure of the tight organization of the self in order to welcome and entertain the impact of the new and unfamiliar idea. Casework does express itself in a new and different language and this too is a sign of its developing maturity.

Casework is a method, a way of helping, not a result or a quality. In its intent and purpose and practical result it is frankly therapeutic. This statement can always be counted upon to arouse doubt and sometimes shock and fear, often projected outward in the question, "But what, then, differentiates casework from psychotherapy?" Actually, the fear is an unavoidable reaction to the character of the responsibility and the nature of the psychological task which the caseworker undertakes. Wherever the difference between casework and therapy may lie, it is not on the score of the value of the therapeutic results. Throughout this discussion from first word to last we speak of a process which aims to help the individual free the temporarily restricted life impulse in order that it can seek out its own natural growth potential, and thus discover the new expressions of self capable of coping with the life reality. The word therapeutic is a life-giving, growth-producing word. It belongs to real life experience, as well as to the special aspect of life created especially for therapeutic purposes. The sense of healing, of unity in contrast to division, of well-being; of the "I," the self whole and unified, is as possible in the common course of a life experience as it is in a process consciously created for this purpose.

But those who come to social agencies are locked in this very inability to discover and affirm the capacity equated with the life element in the self. When we undertake to help, we undertake to create a situation precisely and responsibly established for this purpose. Being an unreal situation, it must be time limited, and because of its very limitation in time, it affords the possibility for the therapeutic results. What this process can be, how it comes about that one human being can use another for the purpose of releasing the source of new life within the self, is the subject matter with which this book deals. Surely it must be said, how serious a purpose this is, what deep responsibility it asks of the one who undertakes it; for as helping persons we do indeed effect change in the one who seeks help, and the only thing which makes it possible at all is that it comes about through his own will and choice.

In the discussion of historical development which follows, it has not been my intention to attempt anything like a complete examination of the history of social work, nor even of the more limited area of casework, during the years under consideration. Instead my purpose is to identify the origin of those concepts which appear and are explored in Part II of this book. By this means, ideas assume the fullness and depth which evolution in thought and practice affords. What is written in these pages attempts to take possession of that which is already known and understood, and, by tracing the development of a concept, to gain the illumination which only the comparison of past and present can afford.

CHAPTER II

THE SPECIAL QUALITIES OF
THE INDIVIDUAL UNIT

THE TITLE of this chapter is a quotation which has singular significance as a focus for this swift view of the developmental phases in social casework across the span of some seventy years, from 1880 to 1950.[1] The words were originally used by a person who had no connection with social work, Secretary of the Interior Franklin K. Lane,[2] who, at the time of his retirement, in looking back at and evaluating the period in which he had served as a government official, characterized the times as distinguished by "the search for the special qualities of the individual unit."[3]

This comment would have gone unnoticed and unmarked in social work history had it not been that Miss Mary E. Richmond, at the peak of her career in 1920, in a paper read at the National Conference of Social Work entitled "Some Next Steps in Social Treatment," selected these words of Secretary Lane to express her own conviction that indeed the progress of social work in the twenty years of her greatest activity had been marked by exactly this search for the "special qualities of the individual unit."[4]

It may seem precipitate to plunge thus into the middle of a seventy-year span of development without proceeding in the usual chronological sequence; yet the reason for so doing is that from this earliest forty-year period, from 1880 to 1920, scarcely anything remains of importance for today's casework practice except this one trend of opposing forces, one side of which is represented by Miss Richmond's 1920 paper. All other facts and details are of historical interest only, interesting for what they were at the time and for the devoted service of many vigorous and creative personalities. But today there survives in social work a similar conflict of opposing tendencies and a vital issue which is the same as that of which Miss Richmond spoke, and the same as that which can be found in National Conference deliberations in every year from 1880 on.

This struggle of opposing tendencies, together constituting an unbroken trend in time, is the struggle between the individual and the social, the one and the many, the psychological and the economic, the inner experience and the external event. The developmental view of social work shows what we have seldom been willing to admit, that no great personality in social work has been able to carry both these opposing tendencies in equal development within the self, but that leadership in social work has flourished through individuals who have carried with passionate devotion either one side or the other of this conflict. One can select from the contemporary scene almost any content in world affairs to examine this same fundamental point of contrast, but we need look no further than social work—can stay within our own milieu —in order to know and comprehend this human phenomenon to the full.

Casework is clearly that branch of social work which carries forward, protects, and lives out in thought and activity the single strand of devotion to the separate, single human self: the worth of the one. Other branches of social work, such as community organization, program making, social action, all by their nature belong to the opposite tendency which places upon the broad program, the external adjustment, the economic solution, the higher value in interest and feeling. Some branches of social work, as yet not so clearly developed (administration, for instance), have not succeeded in clarifying their major identification but flounder in some confusion and problem for this very reason.

The helping person must begin with the devotion to the

psychological at heart, in order to be a helper. In casework, in supervision, in teaching, and occasionally in administration, one feels the dedication to this focus which all the catastrophic happenings in the world cannot dislodge, namely the belief in maintaining life through its expression in person-to-person relationships. Even a lifetime of devotion to this effort to understand in some genuine way the nature of the human self requires a willingness to be satisfied with very little, for mankind has made very slight progress in this direction. But amount of progress is no criterion, nor is any individual in a position to question whether it is or is not enough. In the long run the forward sweep of that affirmation which acknowledges without excessive guilt or apology its dedication to the human spirit in its spontaneous expressions is the dynamic of the caseworker's skill.

To return now to examine this problem in developmental terms, we take once more as a point of departure this 1920 paper of Miss Richmond's already referred to, for in it we find a summation of the experience of preceding decades and a note of bitterness which suggests the intensity of the struggle through which Miss Richmond had maintained her position. In 1920 she writes: "It is only during the last fifteen years that social case work in families has continued to slip from under the domination of the economists. Though case work always demanded a method in sharp contrast to wholesaling, its earlier period was shaped too often by wholesalers. Broad generalizations about relief, about family life, about desertion, widowhood, immigrants, and the rest, served a useful purpose in that pioneer period, but in the succeeding stage of development, case work achieved a more important step forward."[5]

If the dates in this paragraph are examined, it will be seen that Miss Richmond's reference was to the fifteen years between 1905 and 1920, during which "social case work in families" was beginning to establish its own identity. No doubt she knew as she wrote that her own first published work in 1899, *Friendly Visiting Among the Poor*,[6] had played a significant part in the beginning of an epoch in casework development,[7] and had precipitated some of this change away from "wholesaling" and "broad generalizations," of which she spoke.

But the striking fact is that, even in this same "earlier period" to which Miss Richmond refers, there was already ample evidence of the intensity and vigor with which this battle was fought. Even as early as 1886, at the National Conference which took place in that year, Mr. George B. Buzelle, General Secretary of the Bureau of Charities of Brooklyn, was speaking upon the subject "Individuality in the Work of Charity."[8] His was an angry and fervent voice: "We have a vast array of machinery for the production of philanthropic results. . . . And yet the really beneficent results accomplished are painfully insufficient." Continuing, he says: "We may share in plans as wide as the needs of our fellowmen; but if our effort elicit a response, it is the individual who must respond. Through the individual, the wider result must be reached. . . . He must be the principal in action, in his own behalf. We cannot fight his battle for him. He must be the arbiter of his own destiny. He must choose, though he have little discernment. However vacillating he may be, he must decide. He must will, however feeble his will may be."[9]

In the same volume of *Proceedings*, following immediately after Mr. Buzelle's paper, is another entitled "Trampery: Its Causes, Present Aspects and Some Suggested Remedies."[10] It would be hard to imagine a set of circumstances within which the contrast could be more effectively portrayed. In these two articles the approach to the problem is from opposite poles. Both share the same regret that "beneficent results accomplished are painfully insufficient," but the one believes passionately that the objective must be sought through the individual: "He must be the principle in action . . . he must will." The other has no patience with, but only, as later appears so clearly, scorn for, this slow way of working, and searches instead for causes, pursuing them ever more persistently as one cause after another proves inadequate to the task of explaining or eradicating the evil.

Twenty-three years later, in the 1909 *Proceedings of the Conference,* this same theme is once more evident, and again the contrast emerges succinctly in the keynote struck by two individuals who see the problem from opposite vantage points. Mr. Alexander Johnson writes: "In twenty-one years the problem of the poor has passed over from an affair of the individual to one of the neighborhood."

"In 1888," he continues, "preventive philanthropy was just gaining recognition, but the problems of ameliorative relief were the urgent ones. In 1909 constructive effort in benevolence fills the position that preventive work had barely attained at the former period; while the theory of prevention has grown in acceptance until it is a truism to say that poverty is a temporary condition, that it is mainly due to preventable causes, that science has shown us how it may be averted and that benevolence has seized on the method and proposes to put it in practice."[11]

Here Mr. Johnson draws the contrast between that which is "preventive" and that which is "ameliorative," a contrast which was to continue with powerful influence. The contrast became, at times, the vehicle of attack upon casework process. Further, Mr. Johnson's conviction expresses vividly the belief in the efficacy of external, environmental means for the eradication of poverty: science knows the causes, can eliminate them; hence poverty is a temporary condition. What was missing was the understanding and acknowledgment of the equally crucial role played by the individual's own life movement in the use he makes of these environmental factors.

In the same year of the Conference and very likely against the background of the mood and attitude so evident in Mr. Johnson's summing up of the times, Mrs. Mary Simkovitch spoke upon the subject "The Case Work Plane."[12] Says Mrs. Simkovitch, "Preventative work has been considered so largely from the social point of view that the possibilities of its development in what has been called 'case work' i.e., individual effort, have been relatively neglected.

"I think this paper will interest nobody, for I think the modern emphasis is so strongly on preventative work of a social character that case work is secretly if not openly despised. That is one of the reasons why district and family work are conducted with less interest and less capacity than the social preventative work. The general feeling is that case work is a small affair, unimportant, a necessary evil, a depressing piece of business, a practically hopeless job. Everyone's attention is turned the other way."[13]

Mrs. Simkovitch's despair and discouragement are plainly evident, but it is clear that her own attention was not "turned the other way." Moreover, the years which followed were to show that the solution was not so simple as Mr. Johnson had optimistically prophesied, nor so discouraging as Mrs. Simkovitch had pictured.

If time has done anything for us, it has revealed the fallacy in placing so profound a confidence in the illusion of removing "preventable causes" and shows the extent to which this theory obscures the part played by man himself in his own destiny. Actually, this contrast of opposing trends here being examined highlights and focuses one of the most interesting problems with which casework must eventually come to grips: namely, the question to what extent the individual is the victim of external happenings, to what extent he possesses the capacity within himself to choose and determine the outcome. We are now living with the results of extraordinary material benefits provided through law, through program making, and through statesmanship, but still the problem remains, how man himself, the individual, can utilize what is available to his own maximum advantage. Thus this same duality, of external circumstance and inner dynamic, of the mass and the one, continues on in our present experience, as vital as it was in the historical development of social work; perhaps even more vital today, because with the extension of social services the question of what part the individual plays in the use of the service becomes more clearly apparent.

Now we return once more to the point of examining what happened to this same trend in the next developmental phase; what remained in continuity, what yielded to influences of change. One significant fact stands out above all others, namely that, with the coming of the psychiatric and psychoanalytic influence of the 1920's, casework entered upon an accelerated phase of concern with "the special qualities of the individual unit." This concern carried the continuity but at the same time introduced a momentous change in a shift of the center of attention, away from qualities which were environmental and external, toward qualities which were psychological and internal. Interest was greatly heightened by the discovery of man's inner experience, by the powerful desire to explore and understand the emotions and behavior of man.

In retrospect, it is clear to see how Miss Richmond's absorption in the special qualities of the individual was externally focused. The qualities of the individual were sought in facts: in facts painstakingly and finely and precisely gathered, from relatives, neighbors, employers, doctors, lawyers, teachers, and clergymen; from all but from the individual himself, and in every respect excepting this one, there was the utmost regard for him. The theory rested on a search for a solution constructed by the caseworker: the more facts, the more hope that the caseworker could arrive at a sound and valid diagnosis. The more accurate the diagnosis, the greater the likelihood of a workable plan. With a good plan, implemented with sound judgment and a tactful and genuine approach, the goal must surely be reached. As we now know, the one element which of all elements is the most indispensable, the will of the individual himself, was left out of the reckoning. Indeed Miss Richmond had some awareness of this; she referred constantly to her own belief that a change of attitude in the one who was to be helped was the thing which mattered most, but she sought to achieve this change of attitude through direct efforts projected upon the client, frankly and unrestrainedly aimed to effect his change.

It would be hard to conceive of the development of casework without precisely this phase characterized by the fine regard for the external fact, to which Miss Richmond so creatively gave her life's work. In 1917 the fruits of her thought and service came to full expression with the publication of her major work, *Social Diagnosis*.[14] Actually, the publication of this book in 1917 was the end of a period, for already the seeds of the next development in casework, which was to be a psychological development, had begun to take root. In 1918 and 1919, that vigorous interaction between casework and psychiatry and psychoanalysis began to make itself felt.

These developments which came about in casework practice as a result of psychoanalytic influences have been examined with precision, and comprehended in such a way as to become a part of the heritage of social work.[15] A matter of especial interest is how exactly those years in which these influences first made themselves felt can be identified, and how the growth of a professional content falls into clear decades of development. It is possible to see the outlines of the natural and organic time spans of three important decades: the 1920's, the 1930's, and the 1940's, and thus to take hold of and understand as a whole the nature of the evolutionary development in casework thought and practice in these significant thirty years, between 1920 (more accurately, 1918) and 1950. The two chapters which follow correspond to the developmental phases which I have characterized as "The Search for the Therapeutic Factor" and "The Discovery of Function." The development of the third decade is the content of the second part.

But first, in order to give the focus and approach by which this development unfolds, I should like to state the thesis which constitutes, in these pages, the single strand of development to which all detail and factual content are related. It is this: that the important change, above all others, which functional casework embodies, is the shift of the dynamic center for the source of therapeutic results from the helper to the one being helped. From this all other detail of concept, method, process, and content flows. By this statement we do not intend to imply any denial of the determinative role played by the skill of the helper or lack of it; nor of the crucial importance of the helping process in affecting the release of these vital elements in the self. But the quality of this skill does not arise from the caseworker's understanding of the facts and the problem, or from the competence of the diagnosis, or the control by the caseworker of the level upon which the self uses help; nor does it rest upon the accurate delineation of steps of treatment. It arises, instead, out of a primary acknowledgment that the source of understanding is within the self; that here, internally, is located the original upspringing of the impulse toward life, and here lies the control of change and growth.

Today, in appearance at least, there remains a large body of casework practice which describes itself as still located in the same reliance upon knowledge, diagnosis, and treatment that characterized Miss Richmond's method. The only visible difference is the substitution of psychological fact for environmental fact, and therefore to some extent the individual himself plays more part as the source of information. The dominant characteristic of the 1920's was just this emphasis upon the caseworker's knowledge, diagnosis, and judgment—of what was needed, what should be done, and how it was to be accomplished. The new psychological emphasis still consisted of efforts frankly projected to effect change upon another human self.

The origins of functional casework theory and practice lie within this same orbit of influence during the first half of the 1920's. Those who were later to create the concept of function were actively writing, teaching, practicing, within these same early psychoanalytic influences. But gradually there become visible the centers of doubt and the new definition of problem which constituted the dynamic out of which the next development grew; from which eventually the principle of function was forged.

CHAPTER III

THE SEARCH FOR THE
THERAPEUTIC FACTOR

> *Change of mind does*
> *no good; promises do*
> *no good; only change*
> *of feeling will help.*
> JESSIE TAFT, 1927

THESE WERE indeed important and momentous years for casework, this decade between the year 1920 and the year 1930. It was a period of growth for individuals as well as for the profession. The development in casework came about interestingly enough not because of its autonomy as a distinct and separate profession, but because of its relation to a larger, more powerful whole, namely the psychoanalytic movement. Later, in contrast, the decade between 1930 and 1940 (and here I speak of functional casework only) became a period characterized by separation and articulation of difference from psychotherapy, and it was out of this definition of difference that the unique character of casework method evolved. But in this decade of the 1920's the dominant note was still one of unity with another discipline in which the greater strength and creativity were found to reside.

These facts contain more meaning than the bare statement of an historical reality: they characterize the relation between casework and psychotherapy as a relation in which individuals in one profession (casework) used the help of individuals in another for personal therapy, for help with professional problems, for consultation on cases, for formulation of theory, and even for training in their own skill. This is a different conception of training from that which prevails in the current functional point of view, where the source of training for casework lies within its own profession, through processes of teaching and supervision which maintain the unique character of casework as a separate professional discipline. The comparison between this present-day theory and the historical phase in the 1920's is of exceptional value not only because it illuminates development, but also because it adds immeasurably to current understanding of differences which continue into the present with respect to the origin of the theory, the nature of the curriculum, and the source of help essential in preparing to become a caseworker.

This drawing of a contrast existent in current thought takes us a long way ahead of our story, yet requires mention to sharpen the purpose for tracing these developments. The relation of casework to psychoanalytic influence cannot be understood without realizing this fact of the caseworkers' use of help from psychotherapists. This seems to have been the primary channel of influence, although in addition, and not to be minimized, was the interest of caseworkers in the psychoanalytic literature and the rapid expansion of services which placed the caseworker in a helping role in the same setting with the psychiatrist or analyst, as was true for instance in the child guidance clinic movement. Through the referral of clients to mental hygiene clinics caseworkers were gaining new insight from conferences with psychiatrists. Many discussion groups were led by analysts. Caseworkers were attending classes taught by these exponents of a new point of view. Dr. Taft, in 1925, describes the effect of these influences in this way:

"The linkage between mental hygiene and social case work has been deepened steadily and almost without opposition since the inception of the mental hygiene movement a few years ago. . . . Social case work was starving for a practical human psychology, and had been fed for the most part on academic husks. The doctrines of mental hygiene and the new psychology came as the fulfillment of a long felt need."[1]

In order to understand later developments, it is essential first to examine the substance of casework theory in this decade of the 1920's, when it was still undifferentiated from psychoanalysis and when those who were later to become engaged in the development of the theory of function were still within this same realm of influence. Yet from the beginning, despite all that in the 1920's was so much like the traditional psychonanalytic point of view, the writings of those associated with the Pennsylvania School of Social Work and its field work agencies always showed elements of difference. These centers of difference and questioning attitudes comprised the readiness to make use of exactly that psychological formulation of which Dr. Otto Rank is the author.

What casework took from psychoanalysis in the early part of the decade of the 1920's (besides the heightened interest in the psychological already mentioned) was, first, a new realization that behavior originates in sources of inner need and stress, and represents the effort of the organism to satisfy, release, be free of compelling psychic necessity. This realization that behavior is an expression of the human self in its striving to live accorded to behavior of all kinds new value and new respect. Seen as a symptom of emotional disturbance, all behavior, evil and destructive as well as socially valuable, was accepted as an expression of the strivings of the self. The very use of the words "symptom" and "illness" implied that it occurred through no fault of the individual, with a resultant freeing of the individual, temporarily at least, from responsibility for his own actions, since these actions were a disturbance for which he could not be held accountable. This is one of the points of major divergence between the functional psychology and some other current points of view in casework; functional casework has developed a wholly new relation to the concept of self-responsibility, as we shall later see.

In the 1920's the new attitude toward behavior acclaiming freedom from judgmental bias was stated by Miss Marcus thus: " . . . The case worker can eventually accept any behavior without condemnation once she understands what caused it, and that as soon as she can reconcile the abnormal and anti-social with the normal and social, she is on the road to case work."[2]

Revolutionary as this seemed at the time, it nevertheless reflected a fundamental change occurring throughout social work. The direct result of this change was a throwing off of judgmental standards of approval or condemnation of behavior. Much help must have been given and taken in these times with temporary therapeutic results from this kindly acceptance of the client exactly as he was, including every expression of his behavior. It is important to note again that one of the trends which we are following here reflects the developmental changes in this concept of acceptance; today in functional casework theory and practice its meaning has changed in significant ways. Obviously, this historical phase of acceptance was an inevitable component of evolutionary process, but acceptance becomes a sterile and empty concept when it does not move beyond this point.

A second concept which caseworkers took from psychoanalysts in this period was the concept of the influence of the earliest years of a child's life, particularly of the parental influences during those years. Suddenly the whole matter of parental relationships, mother to child, father to child, father to mother, child to siblings, became of utmost interest. Caseworkers embarked upon an endless search for history, an inevitable result of this concept. On behalf of the child, they sought facts from parents: physical, emotional, and developmental; and on behalf of the adult who came for help for himself, they sought to lead him back into his childhood, there to disentangle memories and associations, in the effort to discover the precise spot where something went awry, where traumatic injury occurred. It becomes increasingly clear how intrinsic to and inescapable a part of this theory it is, to locate total responsibility upon the parents—perhaps blame would be the more accurate word to use. For social work was now embarked upon a new era of accounting for delinquency and failure of any kind by assigning the cause to the early home situation. A parent's natural psychological guilt for too total assumption of responsibility finds an ally in this social point of view. Carried to extremes, it obliterates the child's own separateness and responsibility, and obscures the essential acknowledgment that every individual, even when very young, carries some core of self and feels a measure of accountability for his own actions.

Finally, the third important concept which gained support in this period was the belief in causal determinism, and this belief is but a logical and natural outcome of what has already been described. If the trauma occurred in childhood, if the first five years of the child's life mold his character, then there is no other conclusion than that the solution to the problem must be sought in the past. Returning along the pathway to these early years, one must find the cause and correct it. Here, in this sequence of a causal chain, the past holds the key and wields its power over the present. To make this theory effective, the caseworker must be the interpreter —it is the caseworker who studies, assembles the facts, prepares the diagnosis, prescribes the cure and finally offers it to the client. In short, casework found the answer to its search for the therapeutic factor in just this reliance upon isolating causes in the early developmental experience, believing that the promise of therapeutic results arose from the efficacy of explanation, interpretation, and intellectual understanding. By this means it was hoped the conflicted self would be able to throw off the bondage of the destructive childhood influences.

It is precisely with regard to this question of what it is that accounts for therapeutic results that the paths of two schools of thought in social casework begin to diverge and move in opposite directions. In the discussion which follows I have not attempted to carry into the present that point of view originating in causal determinism, for my interest is in describing the evolution of a new concept regarding the therapeutic factor, one which eventually led to the functional method of helping.

At the head of this chapter is a quotation from a paper written by Dr. Jessie Taft in 1927.[3] This brief but penetrating statement contains the essence of the difference with respect to the source of therapeutic results. The similarity between the thought expressed in this paper written in 1927, and the thought expressed in a paper written by Dr. Taft in 1949, is striking: "We can hardly avoid admitting that the help the patient receives comes not from his reliving of an unhappy past but from the fact that he finds courage to live and feel differently in the present."[4] Yet despite this likeness between the two papers written more than twenty years apart in time, there are also some striking contrasts which illuminate in significant ways the scope and depth of development these concepts of helping have undergone in this same period of time.

The first clear expression of dissatisfaction with the lack of understanding of the therapeutic factor is to be found in a paper written by Dr. Taft and read before the National Conference of Social Work in June of the same year. It is noteworthy that this follows her initial association with Rank. What we find in this statement is not only the dissatisfaction with what is missing, but also an effort to formulate a theory: "No one who was using the office contact as his medium of treatment seemed to be very clear as to just what were the factors in the psychiatric interview which produced therapeutic results, and as far as I know there has never been any attempt to establish a clear cut theory of technique based on conscious knowledge of the relation of the process to therapy or case work. We all fell back on the superior insight which made the material obtained more relevant and the interpretation of it more significant; but the therapy, as far as there was any, remained unanalyzed and uncontrolled."[5] The psychiatric interview to which Dr. Taft refers is her own work as mental hygienist in a children's agency, a kind of helping different from the helping process undertaken by the caseworker. In the same paper she offers this penetrating observation: "In my own work I have become more and more aware that the informational content of the interview matters much less than my attitude and the child's comfort in the relationship temporarily established and I believe that in that direction lies the clue to the therapeutic function of the case worker. . . .

"The point we wish to emphasize is that what gives the office interview its therapeutic value is not a rehearsal of misdeeds or a recounting of old loves or fears; it is rather an immediate feeling experience produced by the temporary security which the relation to the mental hygienist in role of understanding parent affords."[6]

This initial formulation for casework of a theory regarding the therapeutic factor, which still remains authentic today, laid the groundwork for later developments in functional casework. The source of influence in the psychology of Rank is evident.

Both Miss Robinson and Dr. Taft have written of the events and developments, beginning with Dr. Taft's association with Dr. Otto Rank in 1926, that led eventually to the formulation of the functional method of helping.[7] These same developments in the growth of theory can be traced clearly and precisely in their own writings, beginning as early as 1918. The continuity of the development is strikingly clear: elements appear which were present from the beginning and never given up; the sharpening of the problem in one year reveals itself as responsible for the next development in another year; the search continues for ever increasing understanding of the concepts at first but partially comprehended. There is readiness for exactly that psychological point of view and relation to helping which Dr. Rank represented. All of this unfolds from step to step in a sequence in which the later discovery of function appears as a natural outcome. Miss Robinson commented upon this readiness for the point of view represented in Rank's thinking thus: "While the point of view here presented comes to me personally and to many other case workers through the analytic psychology of Dr. Rank it seems only fair to point out at the same time that the very rapidity and thoroughness with which caseworkers have assimilated at least certain parts of this point of view seem to be evidence that their own thinking and experience have been moving along the same direction and find a satisfying expression in this psychology. If this is not true, if this psychology does not express the realities of the case worker's experience with her clients, then it will yield to a more adequate formulation. At the present time it offers the best approach I know to the obscure and subtle problems of the relationship between the worker and the client."[8]

This was written in 1930, in the midst of the developments with which we are here concerned; the forecast that casework will need to formulate its difference from therapy comes to pass in actuality, but not through departure from a psychology the essential elements of which were already complete at the time when Miss Robinson wrote this statement.

Between the years 1918 and 1924 the writings of Dr. Taft, appearing principally as papers in the *Proceedings of the National Conference of Social Work,* reveal many of the same ideas and tendencies that characterized the casework movement as a whole. She was herself not a caseworker, in the precise meaning of that word, but a psychologist, a "Mental Hygienist" to use her exact title. In this role she occupied a unique position in affording connection between the psychoanalyst on the one hand, and the caseworker on the other, and undoubtedly carried within herself these interactions between casework and psychotherapy which we have been discussing. Her papers now constitute an important part of the casework literature reflecting accelerated interest in the psychological aspects of helping. During this period her writings reflect the same belief in the efficacy of the caseworker's direct efforts to effect change. In 1918, in a paper entitled "Supervision of the Feeble-minded in the Community," she wrote: "Such supervision (by the caseworker) would do much to keep the feeble-minded child steadily at work—not only because the worker could come in at a crisis to help adjust difficulties and tide him over a period of discouragement, but because the worker would explain the child to the employer and through her ability to adjust problems as they arose would make the employer willing and able to keep a class of workers who might under ordinary conditions be impossible."[9]

The striking change which has come about in the understanding of helping could nowhere be more precisely illuminated than in this contrast between the present-day concept and the content of this early quotation. In recent years Dr. Taft has commented upon the precipitant which brought this change. The child himself, she says, defeated every effort to keep him "nicely put," and brought about from the helping person the inevitable admission that the child's own will had something to do with the result.

It would be possible to enlarge upon the illustration of that which, at this time, showed likeness between the thinking of those who later developed functional helping, and the thinking of casework as a whole. But we are concerned not so much with these likenesses as with the differences which are already apparent and which remain characteristic throughout the whole development. I have extracted four major factors which seem to me to be present in the writings of Dr. Taft and Miss Robinson during this period from 1918 on; factors which carry forward the continuity in this development. These are: first, an awareness of process which consistently rejected the mechanical; second, an acknowledgment of the complexity of the emotional life which led to the relinquishment of interpretation; third, a realization that the self of the helping person was a matter of primary interest and importance in the whole situation; and, finally, an increasing conviction that the compelling desire to produce change on the outside was at its source the desire to fulfill the strivings for change and growth within the self.

It is of great interest to contemplate the part played by each of these elements in the developments which were ahead. For example, it is hard to conceive how the client could have been accorded his rightful place as the central figure in the helping process, if the projection upon him of the helping person had not first been removed. As a later discussion of understanding will elaborate, the longing to understand the human psychic life is first of all a longing to understand one's own self, and if the helping person is not aware of this, the need to understand is projected upon the one who is helped, in such a way that the latter's own self-initiated movement to develop self-understanding is interfered with. The transformation of the will-to-understand-the-other into the more suitable will-to-understand-the-self, is an inescapable prerequisite to the desirable admission that self-understanding is also the aim for the one being helped.

As early as 1919, in writing of the "Qualifications of the Psychiatric Social Worker," Dr. Taft identifies this problem of the caseworker's interest in her own conflicts. The interest of the student, she says, "is bound to center there until she can work her way out. True she is not much good at casework until she has settled herself, but in my experience, there seems to be no way of avoiding this period of subjective interest among students who are drawn from an imperfect world where most people are unadjusted and unfamiliar with mental hygiene. It seems to me this stage of absorption in the personal application of social psychiatry should be allowed for and the objective direction of attention not be expected until later."[10]

Apart from certain implications arising from choice of words, this basic statement of 1919 is still authentic for casework training. The concept of growth, and of conflict as a natural component of growth, had not yet been fully enough possessed to enable Dr. Taft at this time to disentangle the goal of the training process from its association with "maladjustment." Later, her rather regretful concession that "there is no way to avoid this," because of an "imperfect world," gives way to a positive affirmation of the growth process essential for any individual who hopes to use himself in the role of helping others.[11] In 1920 Miss Robinson related this same idea directly to the immediate problem of training students: "For these entering students the most important and most difficult phase of training is their own adjustment to the problems of social work."[12]

In this same year (1920) and in the same paper, there also appears for the first time another element of paramount importance, whose fundamental meaning has not changed, much as has been the development in fineness of detail and fuller understanding. This element is the realization of the dynamic for learning which resides nowhere else but in the one who is to learn: "In my experience, both in learning and in teaching, I have never found a way of 'getting over' knowledge or technique to a person unless that person had a problem to the solution of which that knowledge or technique was necessary."[13] While this idea was written with the specific content of learning and teaching in mind, it carries equal validity for casework, in opposition to the belief first expressed by Miss Richmond that change was accomplished by "direct action of mind upon mind." It forecasts the later exploration of the reality of the individual's resistance to change initiated from without.

One dominant impression which grows from these papers,

written in the early years of the 1920's, is the constant interplay of opposing ideas, actually in movement within the
compass of one paper. For example, in 1920 Dr. Taft gives a
worker-oriented definition of casework which is certainly on
the side of effecting change by direct methods: "This paper
will assume casework to mean social treatment of a malad-
justed individual involving an attempt to understand his
personality, behavior and social relationships and to assist
him in working out a better social and personal adjustment."[14] But before she has finished the paper, she has gone
beyond this into a vigorous acclaim of the dynamic center
within the individual himself: "We blind ourselves to the
primary importance of the dynamic wish, of the will to live,
or whatever you choose to call the energic basis of human
life,"[15] and she has spoken a convincing word for trying to
understand the child *from himself,* not from the adult's projection upon him.

In bringing to a conclusion these illustrations of the elements that have carried both continuity and change, there
is one other concept to be mentioned. In 1928, Miss Robinson speaks of the importance of spontaneity in the response
of the caseworker. It is, she says, in order to be free "to respond sensitively to the changing emotional needs of the
client" that the worker must be helped toward self-growth.
"The movement in an interview is in flow of feeling and
emotion, registered, of course, by all sorts of overt behavior
changes but so subtly recorded that we have little skill to
read them consciously aright. On the other hand we respond
to them intuitively by that process of feeling with the other
person in the total identification with his feeling state."[16]

Here is the precise statement of the importance of "response" in the casework process, later to become the center
of the concept of understanding and to occupy so important
a position in describing the helping process as it has today.
The word "intuitive" gives a clue to the next development,
for it was out of the inescapable question where the control

of the process lay, that the next movement originated. Also, if we were to try to select but one way to characterize the difference that function introduces, there would be none better than to point to the break-up of this "total identification" by the introduction of form, focus, and partialization, through which the client differentiates his own self from that of the helper.

It is no wonder that Rank's concept of the will, his emphasis upon the present, and his understanding of the dynamics of the helping situation should have found so immediate a response in those already at work upon these problems. In 1924 Dr. Otto Rank came to the United States for the first time, and he returned once again in 1926. It was in the fall of 1926 that Dr. Taft went to Rank for help with her own understanding and skill in helping others. From 1926 until his death in 1939 Rank was actively engaged in therapeutic practice, teaching, lecturing, and writing, and during this entire period he was closely associated with the Pennsylvania School of Social Work. It is not my purpose here to restate these facts of his relation to the School, already so well known, but instead to emphasize two important points. The first is the connection between the problems upon which caseworkers were working in the early 1920's as I have attempted to describe them, and the solution to those problems found in the psychological viewpoint encountered for the first time in Rank's creative work. The second is the acknowledgment of the source of this process of functional casework in Rank's psychology. Here we have been examining the developments which show the separation from therapy of casework, manifesting as it does its own new beginning and its distinct nature and character. Yet this casework method is rooted in the will psychology of Rank, from which it can be said a whole fresh psychology of living, as well as a psychology of therapy, a psychology of learning, and a psychology of casework, have emerged. Dr. Taft later writes of this experience:

"Those few social workers who experienced something quite unlike classical psychoanalysis in their contact with Rank were saved in part from the tendency to put into practice with clients what they themselves had found helpful, by the fact that they were not at all sure what technique had been used with them. It was not anything they could grasp and formulate intellectually. Difference they had certainly experienced and were still experiencing, but they were unable to pin it down to anything definite enough to be turned on the clients. They had learned that help comes from something more than intellectual knowing, that it goes beyond the facts or even the traumas of a life history, that it is a dynamic, present, swift-moving experience with an ending; but what to do with it in case work could not be determined so easily."[17]

It is this expression of "what to do with it in case work" which gives us our direction for examining the next phase in this development. That a completely new and unique concept and process had to be recreated in casework terms is evident, and it was to this that the next decade of 1930 to 1940 was to devote itself.

In the field of casework as a whole this decade was the period of psychoanalytic influence, when casework developed from the stimulus which psychotherapy had to offer. It was a period that saw the development of a comprehensive theory of psychological causation, according to the past the determinative power to shape a man's character. But it saw, as well, the beginnings of another evolutionary process which restored the present experience to its pre-eminent psychological position, and gave recognition to the vitality of the human will. At the same time, there developed a fresh acknowledgment of the strength of the human self and its capacity for creative self-determination. The possibilities of therapeutic value residing in the new experience with a responsible helper, and the importance of response, accurate and immediate, were realized. What was still lacking in casework during this period was the grasp of a factor that could provide the control of the helping process. Out of this problem the search for the form—for the control of the process—led to the discovery of function.

CHAPTER IV

THE DISCOVERY OF FUNCTION

THE PERIOD which we have just been examining is a period of intermingling of casework thought and practice with psychoanalytic influences. In the midst of this accelerated change and movement, casework was seeking its own form and identity. Prior to 1930 it was hardly possible to disentangle what was casework from what was therapy. True there appeared occasional reference to the fact that casework did have, and must in the long run have, just this separate form and distinction as method. But this was still more of a hope than a realization.

In contrast, the decade of the 1930's opened with a distinguished event in casework itself which marks the beginning of a new developmental phase, namely, the publication of Miss Robinson's book, *A Changing Psychology in Social Case Work.* Its effect was to gather together and inform with new creative meaning the developments of the decade just coming to a close. Miss Robinson characterizes her own writing in this way: "In the second part of this study, in using the concept of relationship as a basis for interpretation, I realize that I have gone beyond any articulated philosophy of case work; not, I believe, beyond what is implicit in certain trends of present practice. . . . Another ten years and the process will have moved forward."[1]

Past, present, and future are implicit in this statement: the trends in practice, the author's articulated philosophy which goes beyond any yet attempted, the realization of process yet to be. In this analysis of a changing psychology, a new casework psychology was actually created, given form, substance, and reality. By this clarification of what was known the new problem of what was not yet known became manifest, thus rendering itself accessible to exploration and examination. The search for function was the direct result of a new comprehension of this unsolved problem, a problem which we shall attempt to describe. Its solution came about because Dr. Taft, who was a therapist herself, felt the compelling need, in turning from therapeutic practice to the teaching of casework, to discover, now, not the likenesses but the differences between casework and therapy—the separate, unique, distinguishing characteristics of a method which, while related to others, nevertheless was autonomous.

The effect of Miss Robinson's book upon the field of social casework was powerful and far-reaching. It broke up accustomed ways of thinking and practicing, setting in motion fresh new streams of development. In June, 1931, in a review in *The Family*, Bertha Reynolds wrote: "Some books sink into the pool of oblivion without a ripple. . . . Some are like earthquakes, felt but not comprehended at the time and producing no one knows what changes. One only knows that after their coming nothing is the same again. *A Changing Psychology in Social Case Work* bears the mark of such a book."[2] And so indeed it has been. Miss Reynolds adds, "It produces fear, consternation, wonder, deep delight. It cannot be dismissed lightly even though one's fundamental disagreement prompts one to set it aside."

The fear of which Miss Reynolds speaks is an altogether natural and inevitable fear, one which had to be grappled with immediately. It could not be overcome by denying that it existed or that this was a deeply penetrating impact opening up an awareness of the responsibility of the caseworker which could no longer be evaded. Miss Robinson herself takes hold of this whole problem again in a paper[3] read at the National Conference of Social Work in Milwaukee in June, 1931, approximately six months after her book appeared from the press. While the title of this paper interest-

---

ingly enough is "Psychoanalytic Contributions to Social Case-Work Treatment," the substance of its discussion develops the unique nature of casework, just now beginning to find what is its own. Consequently, in order to understand accurately the significance of these developments, the Milwaukee paper must be considered along with *A Changing Psychology in Social Case Work*.

One would think it difficult to select from so much rich content, in so significant a book, any one thing to which to point and say, this was the most significant of all—and yet actually that is not the case. For it was in the new understanding of relationship and its meaning and use both in natural life experience and in casework process that the dynamic for new development lay. In the decade of the 1920's this was spoken of as "transference," a psychoanalytic term, and used by caseworkers with timidity. In 1924 Dr. Taft had written an article on the "use of transference in the office interview";[4] but by office interview she was thinking not of the usual practice in casework, but of a very special treatment process carried on by herself as a mental hygienist in the setting of a casework agency. The transference was the emotional quality aroused in the patient through the very therapeutic experience itself, but for some practitioners its justification lay more in the purpose which it served to accomplish free association with the past. Enough has already been said in this discussion to indicate that, in the different developments which we are here tracing, the "transference" (and in functional helping this word has long since passed out of use) was suddenly realized to be the very substance of the present experience out of which therapeutic results eventuated.

It was with this concept that Miss Robinson was engaged, when she took hold of its meaning for casework practice: "The term 'transfer' is too directly borrowed from psychiatric terminology and leaves the case worker again with a dependence upon another profession and a confused sense of likeness at this point instead of forcing her to analyze her own process in its unique difference from every other professional venture.

"The word 'relationship' which I have chosen here implies interaction and continuity. Further than this it remains to be defined by whatever distinguishing characteristics we can find as we examine the use of this relationship on the part of the client and on the part of the case worker."[5]

The word relationship is still indispensable in present-day thinking and practice. In this discussion of choice in casework process I have made use of it, adding to it another indispensable word, engagement, one which carries some suggestion of the interaction of which Miss Robinson speaks above, and in addition the immediacy of response which constitutes so important a part of the process.

The key point which was absent from Miss Robinson's book, with which she already begins to deal in her Milwaukee paper, was any indication of where the control of this process lay. Her own thinking and writing had gone the whole way in admitting, describing, capitulating to, the primary place occupied by the client in this process. It was precisely this capacity on the part of the helping person to enable the client to feel his own strivings and to define himself in his own terms that afforded the key to the new relationship. The norm, the outer value imposed upon him as a standard and goal with educational intent was gone, and with it control; for whatever else one might say about the worker-conceived treatment plan, it did at least constitute a charted direction, and when this was given up, the absence of purpose, form, and direction in casework process became apparent.

This is indeed a dilemma, for having granted so much control in the hands of the client, where lies any reasonable or necessary control of the process itself? Obviously if the caseworker does indeed feel with the client in identification, as was the essential first step, then what is to prevent both caseworker and client from sinking into the quicksand of the client's confusion and immobility, resulting in surrender to the magnitude of his insoluble problem? That there must be control is evident. And that some of this control must be in the hands of the caseworker is also evident. Since it can no longer be control of the client by the caseworker, then once more it is asked, where is it and what is it? From the core of this dilemma emerged the growth of the solution: the new understanding of control of the process, of control of the elements of the situation in which help takes place; all of this being made possible in new ways because of the difference which function introduces. The first problem for students today is to acknowledge the powerful control which they exercise by virtue of one fact and one fact alone, that of presuming to be a helping person. From this realization the development of the student moves from control of the client to no control at all; then to assumption of the responsibility for the control of the process and of the immediate situation in its form and time.

The precise difference between Miss Robinson's thinking in 1930 and 1940 is illuminated by two quotations which reflect this contrast. In 1930: "First I would make a sharp distinction between the goals of psychoanalytic and of case-work therapy in the extent of the change they hope to effect. A psychoanalytic process disturbs the patient's whole adjustment. In it his most fundamental relationship patterns are utilized and to some extent modified. A new balance grows out of the readjustment experience. In a case-work process, on the other hand, the case-worker may change any aspect of the environment to relieve pressure on the client or to permit him greater opportunity, or she may attempt to change the client's use of a particular aspect of his environment. In doing this, she enters into a relationship with the client which he will use in a characteristic way and in which he will display his fundamental relationship patterns. It seems essential that the case-worker should understand these patterns, but

I would suggest that it is not the function of the case-worker to change these patterns in any radical way. In analysis, a patient is learning to handle his own fundamental problems and the conflicts in himself; in case-work a client is learning to handle a particular problem usually outside himself, in its projection on to the environment."[6]

The understanding of the extent to which in casework, in distinction from therapy, the client's problem is worked out and lived out through projection on the outer reality, is already present in this quotation. This point continues into the newer development; the greatest change in concept comes about in full recognition that the caseworker cannot control the depth of the use of help nor the fundamental nature of the change produced in the process. This is the crucial point apparent in Miss Robinson's writing in 1940: "The word 'partial' has often been used to distinguish change accomplished with case-work help from therapeutic change. True, the definition of agency service and the client's own focus of his problem inevitably and rightly limit and place the problem in partial terms. But no definition and no particularization on the part of the agency can interfere with a client's necessity to place total value on the partial service. Furthermore, when the process of change is felt as inner movement in the self, the client truly risks a total change. This fear of being overwhelmed by his own unleashed forces and invaded by another who has the control, cannot be avoided. It may be reduced by conditions set before him, requiring the breakup of his activity into parts with which he can deal, but somewhere he must take in the shock of the realization of change. This shock involves the whole self for at least an instant in time. It is bearable and therapeutic, not because it is partialized, but because it is met honestly without evasion by a self that has the courage and the organization to meet it sincerely. For this reason I would say that the caseworker as well as the client must use her whole self if she meets her client's need."[7]

The clear evidence of development in understanding of the problem of control in a helping process is strikingly apparent in comparing these two statements, each related to the same theoretical question. Whereas in 1930 Miss Robinson attempted to differentiate casework from therapy in terms of the nature of change—fundamental or otherwise—in 1940 she has come to the opposite realization, that the caseworker cannot control or avoid the client's risk of total change. "This shock involves the whole self for at least an instant in time." And the use of the caseworker's whole self is required. The form within which this occurs is comprised of the function and structure of the agency, constituting the outer reality upon which he projects his inner conflict.

But this momentary illumination of the contrast in time takes us once again far ahead of the sequential story, for what Miss Robinson writes in 1940 is the result of a developmental process during the ten years which separate the two periods of writing.

In 1934 Dr. Taft joined the faculty of the Pennsylvania School of Social Work, and in so doing she gave up a practice as a therapist and an especially focused interest in casework with children. The latter was not "given up" in any sense other than through its integration now with the interest in all other casework services implicit in the task of taking on the function of a casework teacher. But the actual evolution of the concept of function took place primarily in the field of casework with children in foster care, quite naturally, because of Dr. Taft's original and continuing interest in that field. I have already made mention in passing of a fact that I wish now to re-emphasize because of its striking significance. Dr. Taft, who was most instrumental in the discovery of function,[8] and who is today the most vigorous proponent of the theory of distinction between casework and therapy, is herself the person in social work who of all persons had the most direct connection with therapy, as therapist herself, as translater of Rank's books, as writer of an important book on child therapy, *The Dynamics of Therapy in a Controlled Relationship*.[9] If one believes in the compelling influence of an unsolved problem when it encounters readiness in a person to tackle a problem, then here is a precise illustration. For just because of her close identification with psychotherapy, Dr. Taft was impelled to discover the difference, to separate from that which was so dominantly therapeutic, and to find what was unique for casework in order to understand and teach it. And by so doing she made a lasting contribution to the field.

The concept of function was fully developed by the year 1937, when the first volume of the series of Journals of the Pennsylvania School of Social Work, entitled *The Relation of Function to Process*,[10] appeared. Edited by Dr. Taft, it contains her fundamental statement of function which has remained without modification its authentic definition. Today there is not a word of it that one would wish to change. Its meaning is so whole, so complete, yet so compressed, that even for those who believe they understand it fully, there never is a time of rereading but what the understanding of what is written there moves to another level. Simultaneously, in the years when this point of view was being evolved, Dr. Taft was also engaged in major publications, bringing to fruition her own thinking and experience in therapeutic and psychological terms. In rapid succession there appeared, first, in 1932, the important paper on "Time"[11] read before the National Conference of Social Work (a paper which later became the first chapter of a book); in 1933, *The Dynamics of Therapy in a Controlled Relationship*, already referred to; and in 1936 the English translations of and introductions to *Will Therapy*[12] and *Truth and Reality*.[13] It is as if at once two parallel tendencies had been contained in one person, the one an ending phase, possessed in this amazingly productive writing in psychological content; and the other, a new tendency in a beginning phase, of which "The Relation of Function to Process" was the first written expression.

In the Preface to the Journal, *The Relation of Function to Process,* Miss Robinson states: "The problem of the relation of function to process in social case work has been the focus of study and experiment in the work of the case work faculty of the Pennsylvania School of Social Work" for a period of some four years (roughly, from 1933 to 1937). The two volumes of the Journal which followed (in 1938 and 1939) give additional evidence of the great activity in thought and practice which was going on at the school during this period. One other major event in the same development was the publication of the first book on supervisory process, *Supervision in Social Case Work,*[14] which not only added rich detail to the concept of function but also created a new concept of process in a function other than casework. In her most recent publication, *The Dynamics of Supervision under Functional Controls,* Miss Robinson carries forward the concept and method first stated some fifteen years previously and clarifies the universal concepts in which all processes of helping are rooted, at the same time that the distinctive and unique differences inherent in each function are recognized.

This chapter has undertaken to trace the events and publications through which a fundamental change was expressed, a change which came about as a result of the discovery of function and its creative utilization. The problem in 1930 was one of discovering where the control of the process lay; what distinguished casework helping from psychotherapy. In 1930 it was still believed that the caseworker somehow controlled the depth of the client's use of help and the extent and quality of the internal change which he experienced. The importance of the external reality factors of agency and client problem was fully acknowledged but not yet with clear understanding of where the significance of the outer reality lay. From this awareness of problem, explored and worked upon in the teaching process, in the supervisory process, in casework process in school and agency, it at last became clear that form bears a fundamental relation to the process; that the concrete reality of the helping situation carries the true projection of the deepest conflict of the self; and that help upon a practical, tangible life problem affords the potentiality for help which touches the core of the self and sets in motion an authentic process of growth.

This compressed summary has touched upon the question, what was the fundamental difference which function introduced? The question cannot be answered historically or in summary, but only by the full presentation of the functional process of giving and taking help. The whole of Part II of this book will be devoted to the exploration of the nature of this process.

CHOICE IN CASEWORK PROCESS

The ego needs the Thou in
order to become a Self. . . .
OTTO RANK

CHAPTER V

STATEMENT OF THE PROBLEM: THE ULTIMATE SINGLE NATURE OF CHOICE

THE VITAL problem of choice, as it manifests itself in the casework process, arises, interestingly enough, from the very center of the most significant development in casework practice in recent times. This development has already been described in the preceding chapters as the evolution of the full willingness to concede to the one who seeks help the central role in the process; to yield to him the place of "chief actor," to use Rank's words; to see him as the dynamic center of vital forces, imbued with selfhood which carries the impulse and will to determine its own self-direction. This concept lies at the very heart of functional casework and is intimately and inextricably related to every other concept in this casework theory.

Over the years, as new light has been cast upon the client as the central, active figure in a process in which he uses help, various structures in agency setting have been developed in order to focus upon and further the client's choice and responsibility. The most ordinary, most tangible, most seemingly procedural piece of agency way of working can be recognized as an outgrowth of a concept whose roots are deeply psychological. In fact, the inevitability of these very structures as the evidence of the concept of which we here speak is strikingly apparent. The client comes to the social agency which he chooses, to its office, to apply for its services. His interviews take place in the office of the agency, at a designated place, at a regular time. To him is communicated, in a process of initial exploration of whether he wishes to use this service, as much as is communicable regarding the manner in which this particular agency offers its help, in order that he can discover whether this service is for him. By these means and numerous others similar in character, the client's necessity and right to find his own way into the use of this service, on some shred of his own momentum, is safeguarded. The will of a social agency which does not have these structures, or is careless about them, is a powerful unrestrained force, no matter how benevolently intended, that can paralyze into immobility the unstable, unsure self of a troubled person, and sweep him into entanglement with an agency service long before he has any self-initiated movement.

These agency structures—tangible, concrete evidences of a fundamental recognition of the client's autonomy—express the unshakable belief of casework in the concept of freedom of choice. It is the client who must choose whether he wishes to use the help of this agency on the terms on which he finds it; he is the one to whom is left both the necessity and the capacity for disentangling a host of reality problems through which and in spite of which he must act in order to live. No matter how persistently he tries to transfer to the caseworker the burden of telling him what to do, he discovers in the long run how utterly impossible this is. The caseworker, as well, relearns this lesson from every client he helps.

To this human truth, the relation of the caseworker can only be described adequately as a capitulation, a yielding to the way life is, and the way man is made. Words such as "permitting the client to participate," or even the words I have used above, "to concede to the one who seeks help the central role in the process," all carry a serious flaw, in that they imply a possession in the hands of the caseworker which can be conferred or withheld, given or not given, whereas there is no way to escape the incontrovertible fact (and how glad we can be for it!) that only the self can and does control whether it will or will not use help; whether it can or cannot admit another into the realm of innermost conflict and make effective use of the helping person for this purpose.

This belief in the client's freedom of choice in the practice of many caseworkers has been interpreted to be dependent upon the necessity for actual reality choices. If these are not open to him in his situation the casework agency usually feels obligated to provide opportunities for choice in the actual environment. On the other hand, in recent casework practice we have been faced by the arresting fact that help is possible, and not only possible, but profoundly effective, in situations where there appear to be no conceivable reality choices. Now, suddenly, there is a clash, an encounter, between an idea on the one hand and actual experience on the other, a contradiction which cannot be immediately reconciled. Against the background of a mounting desire for greater reality choices, often of an economic, social, and environmental nature, there comes with the force of a new beginning the impact of an actual fact: that help can be given even when these reality choices are seemingly absent. More and more it becomes apparent that even when the necessity for the use of help arises initially through outer compulsion, and even when the person of the prospective client is removed by force from one place to another, even then, help can be offered and utilized in most striking fashion. From this there emerges only one possible observation and conclusion, namely, that choice among a multiplicity of reality factors does not play the crucial role sometimes assigned to it. Hence we are faced with the necessity of examining anew the psychological meaning of choice.

For this purpose it is valuable to look again at the specific casework services that have contributed to this point of view. In respect to the problem of choice these services at first glance seem to be so different in the manner in which they begin, that one would wonder how any common base of method could apply to both at once. On the one hand, there is the group of services characterized as "protective" in nature originating on account of neglect of children, or because of behavior which carries the offending individual into court. All of these services begin involuntarily, and it is out of precisely this involuntary beginning that some of the impetus for examining the question of choice arises. On the other hand, there is the service of so-called pure counseling, where the reality factors of the concrete service are absent, where the request for help is as voluntary as it can conceivably be, and yet where it is evident again and again, in unmistakable terms, that another kind of choice must be remade at some point in the beginning process, despite the appearance of an initial desire for help which brings the seeker after help to the agency. Still another service which has contributed immeasurably to this opening up of the reexamination of the concept of choice is the casework service located at the point of admission to the mental hospital. Here we have the compelling reality that the patient has come, in many instances, against his will, that it is decided by others that he shall come, that he does not and cannot admit the fact that he is sick, and that minor reality choices which may be open to him fade into insignificance in the face of the one inescapable fact that he has been committed as a sick person to a mental hospital.

Here, then, is the situation as it now exists. Functional casework has moved through creative impetus into situations which no one would have ventured to predict could hold any potentiality for effective helping. The administrators, supervisors, and caseworkers who have been willing to undertake these seemingly impossible tasks have gathered into their hands both the potential and the obstacle, and have demonstrated that something can be created to give help in any situation, provided there is willingness to take the situation as it is and create from the given, the fixed, the unchangeable circumstance.

But the answer to this problem cannot be so readily found in any facile statement that a helping situation can always be created in any situation, no matter how discouraging, so long as the factors as they are found are accepted and used creatively. Something else, of utmost importance, must also be present, in order to afford the potential for effective casework help. What is this something else, that can account for the contradictory evidence of our experience? This is the challenging question to which the present discussion leads us.

The key to the exploration is perhaps to be found in the very beginnings of functional casework, and if we look there we come inevitably to examine once more the field of child placement which played so important a role in providing the casework experience in which the concept of function was developed. In this field it became apparent very soon that the child who was to be placed in foster care had no conceivable reality choice in the matter. It was his parent who initiated and carried through this move, and the child who could do no other than let himself be placed, physically at least, so that he found himself in a family of unchosen strangers, in the care of an agency of frightening proportions, and was required to accustom himself to a separation thrust upon him by external force. Under the circumstances he had only one escape, which was to refuse the placement psychologically by any behavior which served as an outlet for the rebellion against the violence done him, contrary to his own readiness. Even a baby spits his food, tenses his body, refuses comfort, and rejects in every psychological way known to humankind the indignity and affront of an alien will imposed upon his own.

The form and substance of child placement changed when the concept of the child's own will entered the realm of helping. For now it was suddenly clear that even though the child had no reality choice with respect to whether he would or would not be placed, physically, he did have, and retained in a way that no one could take away from him, the choice to refuse the placement psychologically. Even though he had no choice of foster parents, he did retain the choice of whether he would or would not take them on as adults to whom he could find a relationship in his childhood needs, emotional and biological. Once this fact was faced squarely, that the child had it in him to refuse placement, no matter how carefully the home was selected or how meticulously he was placed, and when this fact was capitulated to in thought and feeling, then there opened up the promising, fruitful pursuit of the way to create the situation in which the child could discover his own self-created movement. In a word, it was discovered that the casework aim should be to find the way to help the child become related newly and constructively to the inevitable reality factors, at the same time that there was available to him the support of an agency and a caseworker who knew, astonishingly, how to help him bring about his own separation in ways that could transform the experience into a self-willed movement.

From these origins in the child placement field, this electrifying psychological truth moved rapidly into other areas of helping, and soon became sturdily established as a part of the generic whole which forms the common ground in which every functional helping process is rooted. At the same time, when this truth is incorporated into other casework services, especially those dealing with adults, it is evident that an opposite swing has developed, toward more and more emphasis upon the necessity for the reality of the choice. This tendency seeems to arise not so much because of any abandonment of the original principle, but more because of the great difficulty and complexity of maintaining the level of pure psychological movement, and also because of the guilt inherent in holding so unswervingly to the conviction that there is, in the long run, only one single choice which matters in this process of helping. Twenty years of experience give functional casework the right to say that as helping persons we cannot afford to allow ourselves to be misled by the attractive lure of the reality choice. Its attraction seems to lie in an ideology through which escape is sought from the guilt that the helping person inevitably carries.

It seems necessary now to restate the meaning of the single nature of choice. No matter what the service, no matter how it begins, whether voluntarily or otherwise, no matter how much or how little external pressure has been exerted upon the person to get him to the source of help, there is but one crucial moment of time that matters, and this is the moment in which the self chooses between growth or refusal of growth, life or the negation of life; when the organism, in short, chooses to live and turns its energies from the negative fight against what is, to the vibrant immediacy of what it can do, no matter. This is the moment in time that occurs in every process of help, irrespective of difference of function. And while I speak of it here as a "moment" of time, I mean as well a moment which recurs again and again, never to be wholly settled or determined, but in constant process of becoming, as is the life process itself.

While this sounds like a momentous moment, an event of major importance, as indeed it is, its fascinating other-sidedness lodges in the fact that the smallest, most ordinary, most inconsequential actions on the part of the self in the process of which we speak, can carry the meaning of this turning point. This is the mysterious and enchanting way that life is, which provides a unity and connection between the commonplace and the profund.

If caseworkers truly incorporate this concept into themselves as a genuine part of the professional self in helping, then an unrealized potential for helping opens up. In a later chapter we shall be examining in more detail the true significance of content in the pure psychological movement of growth, as intensified in the helping process. But now it is enough to view in its full and true significance the one, single, unadulterated stream of knowing and understanding that comprehends this pre-eminent reality, so essential a part of the make-up of the helping person.

After the whole discussion of casework process has been introduced via the projection of the dominant idea of the new level on which the one choice actually resides, and this has been spoken of as growth or the refusal of growth, an inevitable question and objection begins to take form to challenge the writer upon this subject. Why should growth have anything to do with so concrete a request for help as, say, a request for a housekeeper, a request for child placement, a request for financial help, a request for assistance in becoming established as a new American? Certainly no client who comes to an agency with any of these requests ever comes, by any stretch of the imagination, asking for an inner experience of growth. He approaches this intent more nearly when he seeks out a child guidance clinic, or a psychiatrist, or marital counseling; or he may have some idea of this necessity once he admits, as a patient in a mental hospital, that he is sick. But even in these services, as we know all too well, he soon reveals his expectation that the change he desires will be produced by the other, by external means, or by change in the environment, and he does not know the necessity for inner change even under these optimum circumstances, but has to discover it anew in each situation.

If this be true, how can we possibly speak of choosing help, how can we possibly feel comfortable in offering the kind of service that the social agency offers, when we know so well that the client cannot choose it because he cannot know that it is like this? This is the problem which will be described and worked upon in the following chapter, which deals with the client's initial movement toward the social agency as the first tangible expression of his exercise of choice.

CHAPTER VI

THE CLIENT'S INITIAL MOVEMENT
TOWARD THE SOCIAL AGENCY

> *... The patient's ap-*
> *peal for help is the*
> *beginning of the*
> *process of healing.*
> OTTO RANK

THE HISTORY of functional casework abounds in illustration of the manner in which a sudden illumination of understanding occurs and new areas of potentiality for helping open up when a single new concept penetrates current thought and practice. Such a concept is the one expressed in the quotation from Rank at the beginning of this chapter,[1] and the same thought appears frequently in casework literature because of the meaning it has had for caseworkers. Its apparent simplicity and natural rightness account for the speed with which it was put into use, yet just this simplicity creates at the same time an illusion that this fundamental concept is easily understood and immediately put to the client's use. In actuality, it is an extremely complex concept and one which is peculiarly susceptible to stereotype because of its illusory simplicity.

Stated briefly, the problem with respect to this concept—a problem which we can now see more clearly after twenty years of experience with its use—arises from the assumption, too hastily arrived at, that the client's initial appeal to the agency is in fact and in substance a genuine appeal for help, when in actuality it is never such, nor can it be, no matter how abundant the evidence that he has given the matter careful thought and has chosen of his own volition to move toward the source of help. Not until he has experienced in actuality a genuine piece of what this help is like can he have any reliable basis for choosing, and even then, at every point of crisis in the process, he must choose anew either to go deeper or to take himself out. The beginning for each one who moves toward the source of help is intricately complicated by all manner of circumstances which serve to rationalize and justify the request. If there is any one way of characterizing the function of the helping person at this point, it is this: to help the applicant disentangle his own will to seek and find and use help from all the other wills and pressures and external forces that operate upon him so powerfully. This process of disentanglement he cannot accomplish alone, for if he could, he would hardly need to come for help in the first place. It is this very concrete need which he brings at the beginning, apart from his reality problem, that constitutes the very essence of the first brief experience in using the agency's help and that gives the basis for the emergence of the decision—his own and that of the agency—to begin again, this time with intention to embark upon an authentic and thoroughgoing use of the service that the agency has to offer.

It is my own belief that this process of disentanglement of the will from all the other pressures, this initial period of exploration for the purpose of discovering if help is indeed wanted and can be used, requires the time form of at least three interviews; that it must have a definite and known terminal point, with a decision clearly arrived at. This decision grows out of a realization that a fragment of movement has taken place within a process complete and whole, in spite of its brevity and limitation. One can know with assurance that the client can use help because he has in fact already done so.

In order to understand the problem more accurately, it is necessary to restate and incorporate into this discussion a comparison of two points of view, each of which gives rise to a different series of consequences in a helping process. If the caseworker operates diagnostically, with the belief that he can decide (with more or less factual knowledge) what the nature of the client's problem is, what kind and what level of treatment it requires, and whether or not the client has come to the right agency, then this initial phase is predominantly oriented to fact and to a *prior* decision. From this point of view stems the common belief that it is possible to know in advance to which social agency a client should be referred and that it is possible for agencies to establish lines of distinction for the purpose of deciding the proper and suitable service to which the client should be referred. From this belief many practices originate, such as the endeavor to ascertain from the character of the reality problem and from the degree of apparent emotional disturbance whether the applicant requires a psychiatrist, a family agency, a child placement agency, or public assistance. If the question is honestly faced, one can see how doomed to failure this endeavor is, how fraught with frustration for caseworkers it has always been, and how flagrantly disregardful it is of the client's own choice of a source of help.

In functional casework the beginning stage of the process rests upon concepts diametrically opposite from those just stated. The functional caseworker begins with the belief that it is the client who knows, and that he can be helped to reach this essential self-knowledge in a way that is self-determined. He does not bring this knowledge in any accessible form when he first comes to the agency, but the very application process itself is designed to enable it to come into his possession. With just this much in the way of belief, the helping person has already given substance and meaning to the generalization that intends to "respect the individual," for the most important part of such respect is that it should never lose sight of the fact that the source of healing is within the individual, if he can be helped to reach it; that he alone can uncover and know the problem; and that in the last analysis it is he who holds the ultimate power to use or not use help, he who determines the level upon which he will use it.

Thus far, every word which has been written will be recognized and affirmed by functional helping persons as known and familiar territory. The question then is, wherein lies the problem? Why is this so difficult to accomplish and from what source come the obstacles which at times seem to stand in our way? The difficulty arises because here, as everywhere in helping, the caseworker must carry simultaneously the two-sided character of the experience of choosing, the contradiction, which is the essence of choice itself, until it has been taken back and repossessed by the one who seeks help. Specifically, as related to the particular aspect of the beginning phase which we are discussing here, it is not enough to know that the client's "appeal for help is the beginning of the process of healing." There must also be held in constant relation to this fact its opposite, namely that the initial move toward the source of help is not yet a true choice, and that only out of the process itself comes this new movement, the moment which we recognize as the authentic inner affirmation of the impulse toward life. Students of casework know this movement internally from their own experience. No matter how careful the preparation to come into training, no matter how painstaking and thorough the plan, nothing that happens in advance ever approximates or in any way substitutes for the inescapable choice which must take place, once one is genuinely in the learning process. Knowing this for themselves, students know it also on behalf of their clients.

Some very concrete and particular aspects of this problem require examination, and it is the purpose of the remainder of this chapter to consider a few of these specifics in relation to the general statement of the problem as it has been here presented.

There was a time, in the decade between 1930 and 1940, when conviction regarding the value of explanation to the applicant was at its height. The intention of this explanation was to encompass, insofar as possible, all the conditions implicit in the use of the service: the requirements, the policies, the limitations, the obligations which went with taking what the agency had to offer. The purpose underlying this effort was in line with what we are here discussing. It grew out of a desire to help the applicant choose the service in a more responsible way, in order that he could truly know what he let himself in for if he took something from the agency, either in the way of material benefit or psychological help. This trend toward fuller explanation seems to have arisen as a reaction against a repudiated approach whereby the client was far too rapidly "taken in" without any concrete knowledge upon which to base a decision. But it also indicates a trend toward a new goal, namely, to offer to the client the opportunity for a clear and responsible choice. The locale of much of this explanatory trend was in the public social services, where it found swift compatibility with the legal necessity for utilizing the content of the law and policy of the public agency. However there was also a similar tendency in other functional agencies, always directed toward enabling the applicant to make a reality choice with greater self-responsibility.

As happens inevitably in any development, this reliance upon the efficacy of explanation overreached itself. Too great reliance on explanation tended to obscure the true nature of the individual's relation to a beginning process of using help. The other side of this praiseworthy intention to facilitate choice by means of explanation is the reluctant admission that no one can hear what he is not ready to hear, nor understand that which is wholly outside of himself; explanation can become only an additional deadening weight when it is projected upon the one who is unready.

This realization forced the caseworker to seek for some wholly fresh and creative use of "explanation" in order that the client could in truth know what constitutes choice in the experience of using help. This "knowing" is altogether different from a logical comprehension of the factors, the facts, and the conditions of this situation, as the caseworker knows them.

As the caseworker listens to the client in the application process, the appearance of the particulars in the content of the interviews seems to occur in some natural timing of the client's. The more the helper learns to deepen his own awareness of the other in the interview, the more precise will be his hearing of and his response to those moments of inquiring readiness on the part of the applicant. The characteristic tendency of the inexperienced caseworker is to respond to a question with a factual answer, when often there really is no answer, or when, if an answer were given, it would be rejected by the one who asked for it. If one drops out of attention momentarily the specific content of the question directly put by the client, then it is possible to acknowledge the value of the question to the asker: it may be as the conveyor of apprehension; of doubt as to whether the helping person can really help; of defiance of the conditions which he already senses; of guilt for having come at all; of challenge to the strength of the worker, testing out whether this person has the strength required.

It is always very difficult to put into words the basis on which the caseworker knows whether or not a particular individual in need of help can use the help which the agency has to offer; at the same time in actual experience there has developed a reliable criterion. In essence the conviction forms from having realized that a genuine part of the person seeking help is accessible to, and can be reached by, relationship to the other person. It grows from an awareness that some new element from the immediate situation has been taken in by the client, internalized, and related to in a new way. Every concrete piece of the structure of the agency is an element of this nature. As the client meets these pieces of structure, the fundamental question is: can this person be receptive to this externally imposed condition, in such a way that, instead of pitting his strength against it, he takes it into his possession and utilizes it constructively? In an application process which eventuates in no movement, the client remains solidly fixed in opposition: opposition to these conditions and to the caseworker's way of working, which remains alien and external to his own fixed pattern. He continues to locate responsibility upon all but himself. What the caseworker eventually must learn to recognize with sureness and precision is the moment of yielding in the one seeking help, when the first admission of fault, or flaw, or shortcoming, or self-responsibility—whatever one calls it—suddenly appears and marks the beginning of the capacity to effect some change in the situation through realization of the necessity for change in the self. It is this change, however slight, which can and does happen in the application process, as it must happen again and again in the later continuous process of help.

In short, what we are saying here is that the application process, in certain essential ways, is exactly like the continuous helping process, and that unless it is distinctly and accurately so, the chances are the client will never move into effective use of the agency's service because he has never as yet chosen it from his own self-initiated movement. We are speaking here of a total process which begins at the moment of initial application; which reaches a momentary and partial ending after a time-limited period of three or four interviews; which moves into a new beginning, often with a different caseworker, and thus proceeds into a more lengthy and substantial process, also limited in time. Within that early period, when the reality choice is one of whether to go on with the casework service or to terminate it, the same fundamental dynamics of movement occur. That there are differences in the content and depth of the application movement from the longer helping process goes without saying. But first, before knowing what those differences are, the necessity to affirm the likeness is paramount.

In this initial relationship between the one who seeks help and the caseworker who represents the agency service there comes about a kind of togetherness, a unity, a feeling of understanding, that is commonly spoken of in psychological terms as identification. Were it not for this, the whole situation would be barren and without life, and nothing would ever come of it. Not only in the initial phase, but throughout the process which we are here examining, the concept of identification plays an important part, and it is to this that we turn next as we move now more deeply into the consideration of the nature of choice in casework process.

CHAPTER VII

THE QUALITY OF THE CASEWORKER'S IDENTIFICATION

THE PROBLEM of taking hold of this interesting word "identification" is essentially one arising on account of the change occurring in the quality of identification as the process advances. What can be said regarding the nature of identification in the initial phase of a helping process is quite different from what can be said of it in the concluding phase.

Further, the problem of understanding the nature of identification is complicated by the fact that its quality changes drastically with the development of the caseworker's skill. What we strive so hard to help a beginning caseworker achieve in identification with the client when he is first learning to help is of quite another order from the quality of identification manifest in skillful helping. Yet the very contrast in time, first encountered as a problem, holds the key to understanding, for in the comparison between identification in beginning and ending of process, in inexperienced and experienced helper, lies the opportunity for discovering the nature of this phenomenon which plays such a major role in the relationship of helper to person seeking help.

Still another problem arises from the fact that when we really come to grips with the meaning of identification, we find that our language often states the reverse of what is actually the case, and that we have not yet developed enough precision in thought and speech to convey the important and fine distinctions which have developed over a period of time and do actually exist in practice. I refer here again to the quotation from Miss Robinson's 1928 National Conference paper (which I have already utilized in the discussion of the development of functional casework) to recall the beginning of one continuous line of development with respect to just this change in the concept of identification. In 1928 Miss Robinson spoke of the caseworker's "total identification with his (the client's) feeling state,"[1] and it was precisely this totality of identification which had to give way to admit the recognition of the separation aspect in relationship which is an equally powerful factor.

When the student is just beginning in this process of learning casework, the problem is one of helping him find a way, any way that is natural to him, to identify with the different self of the client. In contrast to this, what we discover when we examine a fine and effective piece of helping is that it is not the caseworker who has identified with the client but the client who has discovered ways to identify with the caseworker—actually, more accurately stated, with the function which is manifest in the caseworker in every step of the process. Hence it seems more accurate to state that the caseworker identifies with his function (not with the client)—this is the primary and elementary origin of identification. It constitutes the steady, unchanging part of a process that in other respects is highly mobile, granting more mobility to the client, to the one seeking help on account of this form. The existent difference between helper and client must be bridged through the client's movement—toward the uniting with the source of help, through his own discovery of partialized reality with which he can identify. If this is so, if it is indeed the client who must create the identification, then this raises a question whether it is ever accurate to speak of the caseworker's identification with the client, when in actual experience such identification can often engulf the client in such a way that he cannot separate enough to present himself in his own terms.

This is the gist of the problem regarding identification and is the approach by which this chapter then considers the question, how can the client thus identify? What does he find in the caseworker sufficiently like himself with which to unite? What brings him back to seek more of what he has already found in prior interviews? If, as we would certainly agree, this immobility of the caseworker which comes about through identification with function is not a refusal, but a highly sensitive response to the client's movement, then how can we describe the situation in order to understand it more effectively?

When a genuine process of helping moves into its ending phase, there can never be any doubt that something of value has transpired between two people. What this is, can, momentarily at least, be spoken of as identification, at the risk, however, of a great oversimplification. There is no mistaking the fact that out of a helping process there eventuates, in slow growth, an experience in which there is a heightened sense of life: as if here, in this moment of time, has been manifest an expression of movement and change like a veritable piece of life itself. What this is, is almost inexplicable, known in immediate experience, and willingly left to be so. It is as if the experience is whole and complete in itself—it needs no tangible proof of outcome to demonstrate its worth. Every person functionally trained, who has in the course of that training been both a helper and one using help, knows, with quickened sense of affirmation, the quality of this ending relationship.

But at the beginning, when client and caseworker first come together, there is no identification whatsoever between these two people. This seems at first glance a most stark and unqualified assertion, yet a moment's pause to look at the beginning situation in its true terms reveals the extent to which this is indeed a fact. The obvious differences instantly apparent in appearance, in manner of living, in life experience, in the very fact that the one is a helper and the other not, are very great indeed. For the young caseworker who is just learning the initial steps of becoming a helping person, the problem is one of finding some way to relate to differences so compelling, for no helping is possible until this happens. Older, more experienced caseworkers, who come into training with attitudes more organized and developed, present in many respects just as keen a problem, but it is likely to be less apparent because disguised as its opposite. An excessive identification with the generalized problem of human deprivation and want is at bottom still but another expression of absence of relationship to the individual. This attitude projects upon him a number of assumptions which operate to his disadvantage because he is prevented from defining his need in his own terms.

Thus, in getting into this problem of identification we are confronted with the necessity of facing squarely the absence of any natural base for identification between two people who now meet for the first time in the setting of a social agency: the one in the role of representative of a helping function, the other in the still undefined position of one who searches for something, as yet not known. One might well ask what it can be which starts this process in motion, what can possibly create the beginning of a relationship from which authentic help may come.

The answer is to be found, in a preliminary manner of speaking, in the realization that only in the willingness to help, manifest in the function of the agency, does the dynamic lie for the initial, original upspringing of identification. It is a matter of paramount importance, which merits careful examination to determine of what this initial identification consists. Within the helping person the function of his agency becomes manifest; in his thought and activity and response, the entity and existence of his function expresses itself. This function is comprised, first of all, of a positive, affirmative desire and willingness to help. Here it stands foursquare, neither timidly nor indifferently, but positively, as living evidence that to this place persons come for help and here help can be given, authentically and substantially. The willingness to help takes on dimension and proportion, form and structure, through a place, a person, equipment, status, and institutionalization, all of which are there, sturdily and reliably, when the individual seeks them out. Familiar and obvious as this may sound, it yet needs stating and restating in order to deepen and possess the full meaning of this willingness. With this willingness the client finds identification if he is at all capable of using help.

The function of which we speak is comprised of many other facets in addition to the primary element of agency-centered willingness to help. There is also a willingness that belongs to the self of the caseworker. There can be no question that the desire to help, enlivened by impulsive elements which strive for creative expression and have chosen this way, in being a caseworker, is of most important value to the one being helped. At times the desire to help is felt so powerfully that it inevitably calls forth a countertendency within the caseworker to restrain and deny, to hold back, to control and refashion this energetic expression. The will to help is a powerful will assertion, and like all will phenomena is bound to arouse denial as its customary accompaniment. It cannot be left unsaid, either, that the projection of the will to help, which we shall be examining more fully in the next chapter, can indeed become pure projection and thus obliterate the self of the client; but this natural fear of the desire to help must not be so great as to interfere with its essential use, for it is an indispensable element in the ability to help.

It happens so frequently as to be suggestive of a universal tendency, that the client at some point early in the process will ask, "Can you really help me?" and the caseworker, in his newness and also in his desire to acknowledge the degree to which the outcome is in the client's hands, may sometimes say, "I do not know, it depends upon you," adding, perhaps a little apologetically, "We have been able to help others." I have never known it to fail that at some point of time in every casework class this very situation appears in a recorded interview, and then it affords a significant point in learning. For now the caseworker examines it to discover that what the client needs from him is the sure knowledge that he can help, the only question being whether the client can use it. No better illustration of the process of differentiation, partialized and concrete, could be found than this. Here the caseworker has the opportunity to separate himself from the client's doubt, sifting it into true components, letting him discover that the doubt is not a generalized vapor which envelopes all—the caseworker, the agency, and himself—but is in fact a limited doubt. What use can he make of it? The knowledge that help is here, and that this caseworker knows how to give it, is the steady unchanging factor, which cannot be drawn into the ambivalence and doubt the client brings. But it is a great deal to ask of a learning caseworker, or even of a very experienced one for that matter, to feel an at-oneness with his function, his skill, his strength, that will enable him to contain comfortably so audacious a statement. Actually the excess of the opposite is justifiably feared, for if the client senses, as he is bound to do, an overemphasized will, "I *can* help," he in turn will be challenged to a will assertion to prove it is not so. This kind of search for delicate balance is a familiar experience in learning the helping skill.

Now we approach the core of the problem of identification, in reflecting upon the question, what is it, indeed, which the seeker after help feels in the caseworker from the very moment when he first begins to work with him upon a problem? How can this be described, and what are some of the common misconceptions with which it can be contrasted? Phrases commonly used such as "respect for," "leave him free to," "understanding of," "staying with him in feeling," are useful but leave much to be explored if we are to understand the nature of this quality.

It is by no means an infrequent occurrence that a client says to a caseworker, even in an early burst of feeling, "This is different from anything I have ever known," and he is right when he says this, for it *is* different. The emotion which gives rise to this exclamation is an appreciative emotion, an expression of surprise, of gratitude, and, in the very act of being said, is evidence of a new-found momentary release as the impulse comes through to this new expression. His accurate observation of difference is not in this instance a separation; on the contrary, it is a sudden uniting, an immediate awareness of having found that which has meaning for him. This is one of the seeming contradictions in helping, that he has united with the difference, yet it is a contradiction which heightens understanding; one of those many paradoxes, the core of which yields the meaning we seek.

For the problem we have to understand here is how the psychologically oriented caseworker, the more or less self-conscious, developed, and creative self of the helping person, can make so immediate a connection with the relatively unself-conscious, nonpsychologically oriented person. This problem is even more evident when one thinks of the highly developed nature of the functional orientation of the caseworker. What, then, is this sudden sense of uniting, of togetherness, of wholeness with another felt by the one who seeks help, which we cannot dismiss as an accidental happening but acknowledge as a matter of supreme importance, without which no helping process can eventuate, cannot in fact even begin?

There is no way to account for this except through recognition of the fundamental connection between accurate and authentic psychological knowledge and the commonplace forms of various and multitudinous expressions of living. Beyond proof one knows there is somewhere an underlying stream which unifies experience, which holds together in some wholly incomprehensible manner the extremes of experience, so that the most enduring art forms make connection with the homeliest expressions of living, and the constantly evolving individuation of the creative person becomes at the same time accessible to the mass. One must believe at bottom that the universe makes itself manifest in every human individual, and the answer lies in finding this connection with the universal at the same time that the uniquely individual is affirmed. This awareness can never be in logical terms and must at times be deeply intuitive, but experience confirms it incontrovertibly.

This highly philosophical observation may seem a far cry from the practical situation of the caseworker and the client. Actually it is not, as I hope to show by describing some of the concrete components of the "knowing" which the caseworker achieves through psychological training, through which, in this same process of differentiation, ever greater individuation and enlargement of the professional helping self takes place.

At the moment of time under consideration here, namely, in the very beginning of the helping process (and presuming always in this discussion a developed, reliable skill), there is no mistaking the fact that the client finds something to which he returns and of which he can make ever-deepening use. In the caseworker he finds a willingness to help, a belief that he can help, and an identification with the function which gives him dimension and proportion in his functional capacity. It is this very difference between the functional relationship and the natural, personal relationships of living, which the client senses. Interestingly enough, it is not absence of feeling to which he reacts, for he finds feeling as real and spontaneous as ordinary living provides—in fact to an even greater degree for the very reason that it has form and purpose and structure.

In the form and texture of this function of which we here speak, there is present an attitude on the part of the helping person for which the word consideration is admirably suited. There is consideration for him as a person and for the problem he brings. It is a consideration which encompasses a special form of attention and interest, a deepened and matured attention and interest, which unreservedly regards him as the center of this hour and place. More than any-

thing, it is a fundamental regard for the freshness and newness and uniqueness of the human experience he brings; a
regard for him at first as a live being, even though at this
very early time the helping person can know so little what
he is like in actuality. But even when he knows the uniqueness of the client so little, he relates to him immediately on
a level which includes more than reaction to the impact of
the obvious outer expressions of himself: his movements, his
hesitations, his compelling necessity to explain himself. The
helping person relates therefore differently from the way
that ordinary living provides, since he relates to another level
of the self which the client brings. Perhaps this can be described as a kind of sensitized waiting and a slow readiness
to feel the client's timing; in short, to feel responsive to this
other self as different from one's own self, capable of being
understood only through its own expressions, not through
imposition of one's own interpretation of what he is like.

Some of this consideration undoubtedly comes about
through the concentration of focus upon the problem which
the client brings, for that is what he has come for, that is
what the caseworker is there for, and as soon as he begins to
project any piece of this problem, and thus projects even the
smallest, most tentative piece of the self upon the caseworker,
he can in turn immediately identify again with that piece of
himself already put out upon the helper. This highly complicated process which we are attempting to explore can and
at times does begin immediately, be it ever so slightly, though
certainly in no manner comparable with the way in which
this constant projection and identification goes on in a developing process.

Highly important to the understanding of the caseworker's
consideration in the initial phase of the helping process is
the recognition of the degree to which the will of the helping
person is contained within the self, not projected outward
upon the other. The word containment is the only one I can
find which seems to approach the description of the differ-

ence between this and the active will which goes out at once in effort to change the other person. Indeed, the will to help is present, but it is a contained will. It may be described as a composite standing-for, an affirmation of, the belief that human beings are capable of change and discovery of new strength and capable of the use of that strength for the solution of tangible life problems. The distinction readily apparent between the quality of the developed, functional skill of the helping person, and the natural tendency of the impulse to operate to effect direct change in the other, is a distinction made manifest in this very difference between the will which is contained and the will which is propelled outward.

In short, it is unquestionably true that one of the facets of difference which the client feels in a helping process is a new freedom for his own will in relationship to another; and this, strangely enough, because of heightened awareness of the boundaries beyond which his will cannot go. All of our language which strives so indefatigably to describe the manner in which he is helped "to discover" whether this concrete service is something he can use is the tangible expression of this mobile process, in which the client's self is left room to move toward ever greater discovery of its own desire, direction, nature, and capacity, but always in relation to a form, a given, which does not and cannot move.

He feels as well the fright arising from this very situation in which he is so unmistakably the center. The relation of two people, in an office quietly set apart for his purpose, where he feels the expectation that from him alone can come the key to the problem, gives rise to mounting tension. This is indeed a frightening situation from which he must inevitably feel the impulse to escape; but this impulse is interlaced with an impulse, as well, to live this out, to go further, to discover what is this sudden sense of self which he feels. The limitation of language precludes the possibility of describing simultaneously two sides of the same feeling, for here, as in so many similar circumstances, it is not a matter of awareness of one side alone, but of the other side as well, and where only the constant maintenance of the duality of the situation can afford the milieu in which movement can take place.

Psychologically speaking, function holds the very essence of this ambivalence, and holds it for the one using help while he flounders first this way, then that, in movements which are now away from, now toward, the source of help. This ambivalence in reality terms is but a reflection of the two-sidedness of the conflict within the self, the very conflict to which he must eventually find access if he is to do anything new in this situation. At first, and almost universally is this true, he unburdens upon the caseworker the picture of the trouble he is in, a picture colored and intensified by the fact that he has been preparing himself to come to this agency. His reverie in advance is the kind of reverie that we all know when we ready ourselves for an encounter: he argues, he explains, he justifies, he excuses, and he usually has a temporary and hasty solution. The caseworker includes this in a larger whole, one which feels the mounting tension of his coming, which feels his dire necessity to tell it the way he has thought it out before he came, which feels at the same time how inevitably he fails to say it just the way he wants. At least two additional factors of major importance the caseworker knows: that his compelling necessity will be to locate the responsibility for the problem entirely upon the outside, and, secondly, that he will conceivably exaggerate the problem because of his intense need to project it upon the other, in fear that the helping person will not understand it truly, as he does not himself. Within his function, within himself, within his agency concept, the caseworker can respond to the intensity of his feeling while withholding himself from engulfment in the overwhelming impact of what great misadventure he has had, for it is this very engulfment and its totality with which he most needs help. If the caseworker

goes into it with the client he fails to give him just the help
that he needs.

It is this accretion of sympathy which is the snare and pit-
fall of the helping person. All too often the reality suffering
is indeed so great, the misfortunes which befall so unbeliev-
ably weighty, the combination of deprivations and accidents
so overwhelming, that it is a wonder the client can feel anything except complete defeat. But the caseworker does indeed know this: that if this human self is to find any shred
of capacity to cope with what has happened to him, he must
also be able to find the germ of a sense of self-responsibility.
For it is too obvious to escape notice that despite the pre-
ponderance of excuse, of rationalization, of blame located
upon the outside, at bottom he feels his own part, and feels
it with inevitable guilt. What he craves above all else, yet
does not reach in accessible form, is the recognition that he is
not the victim of circumstance but a responsible agent even
with respect to acts and attitudes which he finds blame-
worthy. Only the necessity of fighting the helping person, to
impose his own will in opposition to the pressure which he
feels externally, will interfere with his sure movement to
reach this admission and to give it, as a genuine piece of
the self.

Later, in far more detail than is possible here, the whole
concept of self-responsibility as it expresses itself in functional casework will be examined with more care. Now it is
enough to mention it in order to include it within the scope
of this condensed exploration of the nature and meaning of
the function the helping person contains. It is a function
which comprehends the opposites of self-responsibility and
external inevitability; which knows the universal tendency
to come for help bearing the compelling necessity to say: see
what has "happened" to me; which accepts this, but does so
within a larger whole containing as well the knowledge that
location of responsibility must move from outer to inner, if
growth is to be the outcome.

Sympathy is an emotion that gives meaning to natural human situations, but it is not very well understood with respect to its part in professional relationships. What is at least clear, is that the nature of the positive feeling present in the helping situation is of a different quality and upon another level. On occasion, however, the emotion stirred in the caseworker is more of the quality of sympathy than otherwise, static as an emotion on that account. Sometimes, along the pathway of learning how to help, even this emotion, when it is real, is welcomed as a thoroughly valid and authentic expression of feeling, but in and by itself it engulfs the caseworker in the client's problem, and the only resultant change is that there are two involved instead of one. I do not mean to belittle the moments of helping which seem to eventuate from nothing more than a kindly reception of a troubled story, an experience psychologically comprehensible as the relief which arises from momentarily uniting with another, thus softening the feeling and liberating the armored will. It is true that wonders can happen from just this very instantaneous unity which causes the fear to subside. But it need hardly be added that no genuine beginning of a self-movement toward growth eventuates from this sterile uniting in sympathetic feeling. Actually, sympathy soon deteriorates into feeling-sorry-for, and being-felt-sorry-for is closely akin to being-looked-down-upon, and therefore soon is felt as an affront.

The movement in learning to help is characterized, first, by an awakening capacity on the part of the student to feel for the self of the other, and any kind of real feeling—concern, sympathy, anguish—is welcome and indispensable evidence of change. This capacity must develop into a slowly growing ability to contain the two sides of the immediate situation, that is, the feeling for the person he is, and also the feeling for the better self which he might be but is not. Of all the aspects of this helping function with which the caseworker holds her identification in the early contact with the client, perhaps none accounts more meaningfully for the fact that the client knows there is something here and returns to it. In nonconceptual, nontheoretical, nonconscious terms, intuitively and immediately he knows this enlargement even though he cannot yet own it or possess it for himself. Toward this expansion the self stretches and reaches, beyond its known limits.

In concluding this chapter, we come back once more to look again at the nature of the caseworker's identification, and see it as primarily an identification with his function. In order to avoid the surface connotations which these words sometimes imply, this discussion has sought to put detail and content into the nature of that function which is informed with meaning through the caseworker. What is described here could never be spoken of as an "objective" attitude, excepting only as it remains centered upon the "object," in this case a living human self. On the contrary, it is a vital, dynamic experience, in which the fear of feeling and emotion is contained within form and thus loses its power to obstruct expression and movement. The whole development from undisciplined human being to disciplined professional helper can be described in part as a process of becoming aware of one's own emotions more accurately and immediately in order to respond precisely and genuinely to those of the other. The opposite of this is the fallacious but commonly held ideal of the caseworker as one who is objective, "free" of prejudice, "free" of judgmental attitude. Actually, the more the self grows, the more it is full of emotion, the more sensitively it responds, the more spontaneous it becomes. It is a matter of affirming, containing, recreating, the self, courageously and spontaneously, in order to learn to help.

In the next chapter we shall once more take hold of one facet of this problem, namely, the will to help as it manifests itself in the caseworker, and examine its nature as it expresses itself in the helping process.

CHAPTER VIII

THE WILL TO HELP

W HAT IS the nature of this will to help and how can it become either an effective dynamic or an equally effective obstacle to any constructive movement on the part of the client? These are the questions which must be explored, for the will to help is, in all certainty, a very powerful force, little understood and very often denied; feared because of its strength and the responsibility which it places upon the helping person.

Once again there seems to be value in examining this problem through the comparison of different points in time, as revealed first in the natural self of the casework student seeking training, then in the developing self in learning, and finally in the mature self of the experienced caseworker. For in these three points of time, which correspond to the natural eventuation of a growth movement, are to be found the authentic outlines of the maturing will to help as it eventually manifests itself in the skillful caseworker.

This brings us inevitably to the interesting question of the motivation which brings any individual into casework, into the choice of a helping profession, and into the difficult and painful process of self-development which any ability to help demands. Only a very deep devotion to the intrinsic worth both of the own self and the other can account for undertaking a task so demanding and so fraught with pain and pleasure alike.

When the original and most accessible motivation which brings a caseworker into training is first expressed, it contains often a considerable emphasis upon the desire to contribute to the well-being of the world. Usually the individual describes some point of impact when the realization of human suffering, material and emotional, was first felt, and not infrequently he can identify some actual event in his personal or professional experience which set into motion the incipient desire to change the situation as he finds it. The preponderant characteristic of this early expression of desire to help is a desire to change the outside, not only the environment but human beings as well, for it is likely that the average caseworker who comes into training with any experience (and even the young inexperienced student who has been stirred through college courses devoted to social and economic issues) sees not only the potentiality for change in the environment, but also the promise of change within the individual human self. Whichever way he looks at it, whether in terms of the broad sweep of human progress, or centered in the single individual, it is the effectuation of change upon the outer reality that constitutes the drive out of which the interest arises. When he comes into training, in contrast, he discovers that the center of change is within himself.

Furthermore, combined with this desire to be active on behalf of human welfare, there is usually an equally power- ful expression of interest in understanding human behavior; in fact the latter seems to become the next step into which any discussion of the question, "What brings you into train- ing?" inevitably leads. There is no escaping the realization of the universality of this craving to understand the way human beings are, what they do, and why they do it. The association between the thought of being able to help and the necessity to understand human behavior is clear and direct.

But now, what is here described is soon discovered to be merely the surface manifestation of a motivation deeper in origin and more complex in nature than is apparent at first glance. Under favorable conditions not very much time is required in the training process before the learning self finds new ways to admit, "I want something for myself," and "It is my self that I crave to understand." These two admissions, felt at first as too self-centered, and needing to be denied on account of the guilt aroused, are suddenly acknowledged as authentic parts of the self that can be accepted and included and to some degree satisfied. In this very realization an important part of the training movement of the student eventuates.

In order to go into this problem even more penetratingly, it is necessary to consider as well the creative strivings of the individual who comes into casework, strivings to use the self more effectively, to find channels of expression that satisfy; to live out whatever of capability and potentiality is felt to reside within the recesses of its being. Perhaps "creative" seems too pretentious a word for these common, universal strivings, reserved as it is for characterizing the higher forms of art. Yet there is no other word which seems to carry this same meaning, when one undertakes to speak of the kind of creative expression which is actually life experience itself. At the heart of Rank's psychology lies the belief that life experience is and can be creative, and that the striving for growth and individuation is in itself an expression of the creative impulse. The same thought has been philosophically comprehended in recent times by Bergson, Dewey, and others. The individual who selects casework as a profession is likely to be one with more than average awareness of himself and his difference, and more interest in, and sensitivity to, experience. The striving for creative expression brings him into a helping function, where he does indeed discover, if he develops any skill at all, that in this medium it is possible to find form and use of himself to the extent of his capacity. L. P. Jacks calls it "skill-hunger": "Man is a skill-hungry animal, hungry for skill in his body, hungry for skill in his mind, and never satisfied until that skill-hunger is appeased."[1]

Thus we begin to identify some of the important elements

of the will-impulse combination which brings the individual into the choice of a helping profession: desire for skill, striving to understand the self, pressure to live out the endowments of the self, and a compelling will to change, to recreate, to make over the outer reality in which he lives. These now stand at the threshold of new understanding, to be seen either as the static, resisted, denied elements in helping, or the accepted, affirmed, and therefore constructively used elements in this so fine and precise a task.

When the desire to help in its unformed, natural, undeveloped state is given free rein in social work, it becomes a powerful projection of unassimilated and unrecognized pressures within the self of the would-be helper. Under these circumstances the client becomes an object—an animate one, to be sure, but an object nonetheless—to be observed, studied, interpreted, and diagnosed. The longing to understand one's own self thus seeks the answer through the effort to understand the other. The tremendous dynamic of the will to change seeks its satisfaction by way of the mounting desire to produce change externally. Parts of the self felt as problem are seen in the other. The inner stresses and conflicts which are the natural substance of any life process are mirrored everywhere in the environment, and the impulse to effect change begins to operate with this compelling drive.

Beneath this activity, propelled outward upon the client, lies a theory which is in itself a powerful projection. It is a theory with respect to the method of producing change in the one who seeks the caseworker's help. According to this theory, the change happens as a result of the caseworker's understanding: of causation, of the client's problem, of the solution. Centrifugally, diagnosis originates and continues to be centered in the caseworker, even while it is directed outward with purpose. It can be successful only if the client takes it over organically and makes it his own. It is hard to see how this can ever happen, knowing the inevitable reaction of the will to projected pressure of this kind. More likely the truth is the client fights to the last inch the imposition upon him of another's interpretation of where his problem lies, what its nature is, how it came to be the way it is, and where its solution can be found. Sometimes, in fact, the necessity to fight is so great that the very energy thereby generated motivates him to produce some change in his situation in order to escape and by this means he uncovers new sources for self-responsibility. But this is a far cry from a reliable way of helping because the change springs from opposition and does not necessarily become a part of the self.

Against the background of this contrast it is possible to comprehend and examine, in its sharp difference, the process of development which the powerful will to change the outside, as it first appears in the natural self of the student, can undergo in a true process of inner growth. The desire to understand the mysterious and alluring realm of psychic phenomena, constituting as it does the primary desire to understand the self, is admitted, acknowledged for what it is, and accepted in the sense that it is confirmed positively, not negatively as something evil which ought not to be. It is, which is enough. Gradually, but from the very outset, the functional training process supports and encourages this willingness to understand the self, and uses every facet of the immediate experience, commonplace and momentous alike, to deepen and enrich the comprehension of the self in all its impulsive and willful and self-striving assertions. Once this desire to understand the self begins to be satisfied, as it cannot ever wholly be, but only relatively speaking within the possibility of the present experience, the projection upon the outside becomes amenable to a gradual return and taking back into the self where it belongs. The creative urges for change also become transformed into a will to have the change occur internally, now felt less compulsively, with less determination, with less of a preformulated goal; and the sense of mounting inner strength, as well as outer strength in the help available to the one learning casework, frees the willingness to live out a process, step by step, day by day.

To express this change in the self we resort once more to the use of the word containment. Strength becomes contained, and through its containment enlarges. Bit by bit the artificial strength heretofore clung to as essential, serving as an armor intended to afford invulnerability against the onslaught of life reality, is given up for the enhanced awareness that man is indeed a vulnerable creature who lives in fear and danger and change and flux. It becomes evident that if one can but know this life reality, can go with it and live out its very precariousness in change and process, then truly, and only then, can life find genuine expression.

Now, too, the powerful will to create, to change the material things of the environment, is no longer rejected as evil, but takes its rightful place as a part of the creative urge itself. And through this realization, the growth process finds new impetus.

If the will to help can become contained and affirmed within the self, it no longer drives out upon the client in sheer projection. Since it does not threaten him, the client can move toward it, to discover what is there which he can use. This strength in the helping person, which we have characterized as an inner strength, is immediately felt to be different from the kind of strength which depends upon knowledge about the other or resorts to a complex and elaborate system of causal explanation. In relation to this inner strength, the individual who seeks to use it becomes more aware of his own, in comparison and contrast, in awareness of difference, in sense of likeness, in give and take and engagement with another human being. He knows the character of his own will through engagement with the will of another, when the focus remains always devoted to enhancement of his own understanding.

Yet another related concept becomes illuminated at this point, the importance of which it would be impossible to exaggerate. At bottom, as the substratum of every effort to help, is the solid belief that only the client can know himself from himself, and that any understanding worth its name is self-understanding. To be sure, the individual client can be known by another from the way he is in a relationship, the way he acts, speaks, responds, moves, resists; by the admixture of will, impulse, fear, and guilt which manifests itself under these particular circumstances, but in the last analysis this knowledge is partial and transitory. The caseworker in the training process knows this for himself in the help he has used: the goal is self-understanding, and the only acceptable truth is the inner truth of the own self. What the helping person puts in to facilitate this understanding in terms of acceptance, immediate response, awareness of past and present, in terms of psychological movement, are all particulars of the same problem which we shall examine in more detail later. But taken all in all, one always returns to this first elemental affirmation, that the self can only understand through an immediate experience and new comprehension of itself. That one can be helped toward this goal in substantial and responsible ways is the conviction out of which any person undertakes to help. Here we describe once more a duality, a two-sidedness of self and other, which the restrictions of language cannot altogether convey simultaneously, but which fortunately the helper can contain in immediate awareness in simultaneous juxtaposition.

In bringing this chapter to a conclusion, it is necessary to refer to one other fundamental factor in the will to help, and this can only be mentioned, since it requires fuller development in order to do it justice. This factor is the essential engagement of the will of the client in order to effectuate any helping movement. Even experienced helping persons back away from the full realization of the extent to which two wills are engaged in the helping process. The reason for this is not hard to find. What the helping person aims to avoid at all costs is the kind of will struggle which sharpens to that

ultimate point of encounter between two powerful forces—
the one in the helping person, the other in the client—the
outcome of which can only be defeat, no matter which will
triumphs. In this situation, the client can use his whole
strength only in refusal pitted against force; stated in pure
psychological terms, in counter-will in opposition to the
powerful will which he meets in the caseworker. This occurs
even when the content of the caseworker's powerful will is
composed solely of benevolent intentions.

Yet this fear of the will struggle, if the fear is excessive,
restrains the caseworker from that very encounter with the
client which is indispensable and which the client will surely
seek dynamically if anything in the process has touched him.
The fear on the part of the helper is unavoidable; it is a reality that exists and cannot be changed. What can change is
the caseworker's relation to the reality.

The connection between will and fear is direct and immediate. Will is a means for conquering fear, and at the moments of keenest will assertion—sheer will stripped of feeling
—fear is not felt or is felt as under control. Let the fear well
up and it threatens to take possession of the self. In helping,
it can be accepted as axiomatic that the greater the fear, the
more the will sharpens. This continues to be true for the
client, although in the process of using help it too can be
modified. But for the caseworker the training process precipi-
tates change with respect to the will-fear connection. Where
there is genuine psychological growth there is increasing
capacity to feel the fear with resultant decrease in the necessity for will to control. The functional helping situation is
set up with a structure designed to permit the client's fear
to be released and felt, something which ordinary life seldom
affords and which he can hardly venture alone without risk
of loss of life. Actually the self can choose to feel the emotion,
even of fear, and thus be the possessor of the emotion, rather
than the other way round: the emotion possessing the self.

For the helping person, the answer to this problem of the

accentuation of will by fear is to be found in the change which occurs in the growth process. The fear is contained within a larger whole comprised of self-awareness, which includes the awakening realization of the constructive, life-producing aspects of the human will. When the convincing evidence that emotion felt and acknowledged does not engulf and destroy, but frees and creates, has been experienced again and again, the fear of the emotion actually diminishes.

It is to a deepening comprehension of this process that the following chapters are devoted.

CHAPTER IX

THE MEANING OF ACCEPTANCE IN THE CASEWORKER'S RESPONSE

T HE EXAMINATION of the will to help has served to concen-
trate attention upon but one of many aspects which
might be assembled to construct an answer to the question,
"What is a caseworker made of?" We have just seen how one
must acknowledge that a caseworker is possessed of strength,
and, having strength, has a will, and having will has an urge
to create, that is, to change what is, in the image of one's own
idea or conception. And we have said that, in order to avoid
the devastating effect upon the client of sheer projection of
this will to change, the impulse-will organization of the
would-be helping person must undergo a development and
growth, in the process of which the projection is taken back
from its exaggerated location upon the other, to ever greater
containment within the self. This resulting containment is
quite a different matter from a contrived control of strength
through a decision of the will; is in fact just its opposite,
since a denial of its existence or a repression of its strength
constitutes a flaw which interferes with any effective effort
to help.

It is on account of this very sense of strength and creativity
in the helping person, manifesting itself more deeply and
more powerfully than is ordinarily the case with the average
person, that it is possible to understand its opposing tendency, namely, the need to deny that this strength does in fact
exist. At times one sees the profession of social work paint-
ing a picture of its individual practitioner as a person who
is essentially non-judgmental, non-moralistic, unprejudiced,

and pre-eminently objective; free of any reactions of surprise, shock, blame; unencumbered by standards of value, or criteria of right and wrong. The caseworker, it is said in a wholly false use of the word, "accepts" the client as he is, with implication thus of a most misleading use of a very useful and indispensable word. For acceptance is indeed a word full of movement and life provided it is imbued with the concept of constructive acceptance; but it is a word which can also be used destructively when called upon to justify a static acceptance of the client's immobilized self, and this comes about through excessive identification with his misery, or fallacious excusing of his behavior. This contrast between the two possible uses of the word constitutes the focus in this chapter: how to undertake to comprehend the difficult and fine distinction between acceptance that is sterile and acceptance that constitutes a dynamic in the caseworker's attitude.

One might well ask, too, what it is that happens to all the prejudices, the morals, the ethics, the standards of behavior, and the feeling reactions which the caseworker certainly shares in common with all humanity and clearly cannot dispose of by throwing them away, merely by an act of will. If one were satisfied with the picture of the objective social worker described in the paragraph above, one would indeed be satisfied with a human being who had lost all humanity and all self; and a deadly thing it would be! Instead, it is apparent that just the opposite must be true, if we accept the fundamental thesis, as this whole discussion does, that the caseworker should be a person of some unique endowment who undergoes greater than average self-growth and individuation in the process of preparing himself to become a helper. Then, clearly, this person who has consciously chosen development becomes a person with more will, more creativity, more and richer emotion, freer impulse, finer discrimination, more mature values, and a greater desire to use all of these in some more freely experienced existence. What a strange thing it is, this necessity at times to repudiate these parts of the self, or at least to compartmentalize, so that the client is deprived of the very thing that alone can make helping worthwhile, namely, the use of the whole strength of the helping person.

It is a fundamental concept in functional helping, and a fundamental tenet of functional training, that the learning self must be enabled to discover and release and utilize more and more of its growth potential, and, through use, to facilitate integration. But while this is fully understood and acknowledged, it is by no means an easy matter to draw the distinction between acceptance as descriptive of an attitude of the helping person which includes and utilizes all that he is and thinks and feels, and acceptance which denies and obliterates these same living currents of the self.

For if now, without stint or reservation, we are to come to grips with this problem of the meaning of acceptance, we are confronted once more with an inescapable starting point located nowhere else but in the helping person himself. We can begin to understand acceptance through some consideration of its meaning in relation to the own self, since we speak of the process of growth as comprising a process of acceptance of the self. Through this acceptance, the helping person in turn is enabled more effectively to accept the self of the other, and then to help the other to accept himself more fully, thus gaining more capacity for coping with reality. These are the essential facets of acceptance which play back and forth in interaction upon one another, and none of them can be omitted from a consideration of the meaning of this concept.

At first the characteristic mood of the beginning student in arriving momentarily at acceptance of the self is one of relief, as if now the necessitous struggle to become different, to be hospitable toward strivings for change, can, temporarily at least, be given up. The inner conflict of the self (and by this we mean not the extreme conflict of the neurotic but the common, usual conflict of any ordinary life process) is beneficently put to rest, and the self becomes whole in some new sense of "I." At this stage the self must struggle anew between the forces which strive to maintain the status quo, holding on to the past and to the old self, and the forces which strive for change and development. Soon it is all too plain that acceptance of the self is no complacent, relaxing settling down with the way things are.

For, in essence, the gist of acceptance of the self resides in an unfolding willingness to permit the denials to drop away, and not only this (somewhat passively stated as "letting drop away"), but also a fresh active acceptance of the desire to be aware, in the moment, of the true feelings and the true circumstance, no matter what they may reveal. Less and less does the proud self need to create an illusion in order to mask the true situation, and more and more does it place higher value upon the authentic and accurate awareness of the passing moment. Indeed, this is but a description of an ever continuing process, once more calling for the reminder that it is never thus completed or achieved, but always in process of becoming.

In the most general terms one can say it is a matter of accepting one's self as human, which, strangely enough, most human beings find it extremely difficult to do, and even those who believe they do are often enough only caught in other deluding denials. At each new point of acceptance of the self, as within a newly created vortex of energy and life, there is set in motion once again a new process of deepening acceptance. It is possible to describe what comprises some of these centers of acceptance.

To accept one's self means to realize the nature and extent of the impulsive elements and the degree to which, in the creative person, the impulsive elements become ever more rich and more powerful. A change begins to take place when the older attitude which so deeply feared the impulse is given up, and the self is freed from the struggle in which it was forever engaged, striving to restrain or repress this ever upsurging original life. The more the impulse is fought, resisted, denied, the less the whole self can be free or integrated, for it can easily be seen how much strength must go into this conflict. With the awakening recognition of the impulse as life-giving, life-creating, there comes immediately an inevitable fear, not to be explained away or otherwise got rid of. The only question is, can the fear be encompassed and contained and utilized constructively. There comes, as well, a crescendo of desire to release the impulse: freed from the constricting nature of fear, affirmed as right, even wondrously viewed as the stuff of living itself, the forward urge is to live out the impulse. Here it is spontaneity alone which matters, and the self is stirred with an intense desire to live, to give out, to spend itself to the utmost. Yet still another stage, if the development proceeds and comes to full fruition, is that in which there is new unity of impulse with will, in which the impulse feels its spontaneity, but springs now out of sturdy roots; when freedom comes not from license or lack of form, but through that form of self which is only to be achieved through a long, slow process of growth. For now the impulse becomes contained in the service of the whole self, and the creative will molds it and gives it direction. There is new readiness to capitulate to the compelling truth that formless spending of the self is but of transient meaning and never seems to hold the answer to the search; that only in form, in function, in a discipline sometimes felt to be as rigid and unyielding as any outer limit, can true creative expression be found.

To accept one's self means, as well, to acknowledge the own will, and this, in turn, means the acknowledgment of many concrete partial expressions of the total will. It means to acknowledge within the self a high degree of self-responsibility: no longer can it be a question of "what happened to me," but what I myself created through a utilization of external circumstance and inner willing. All of the so-persistent, so-continuous, so-deluding denials of the will expressions of the human self begin to drop away, and a new awareness of inner strength grows. This is bound to be fraught with both exhilaration and anxiety, for it means both the release of energy and the admission of self-responsibility. It is an electrifying moment when the self first admits, and then acclaims, a sense of "I." I think, I feel, I will, I am of worth, a part of an existing whole. I am responsible, says the new self; I am not a mere product of all that has happened to me in the past, nor of the blind instincts which rule me from the mysterious, labyrinthian recesses of a hidden unconscious. Over this moment I hold some potential for choosing and directing my own destiny. This is the meaning, be it ever so partially stated, of acceptance of the self.

Further, to accept one's self means to admit into the realm of respectability—not merely tolerated, but welcomed—the determinative role played in life by the emotions. To accept one's self as human means to acknowledge and go with this primary fact, that man is made of emotion; and the wonder is that he has had to be so fearful of it, so guilty for it, so denying of it. The acceptance of the emotion is the key to the opening of more acceptance of the self, and opens as well the possibility for seeing what is so unmistakably there before us if we would but see it, how the emotion and the intellect are not separate faculties but in constant interplay and interaction one upon the other.

To accept one's self means to admit for one's self that the ideal of goodness in one-sided isolation is a false and sterile ideal because it denies the whole reality of life. The nature of man is such that he contains within himself two equally powerful forces: one positive, one negative; one constructive, one destructive; one loving, one hating. This two-sidedness of the self is what demands acceptance. There are times when the helping person knows beyond doubt that what the client craves is to be felt really and accurately, bad as well as good; when, in fact, he seems to want above all else that the other know the less admirable side of himself as well as the admirable; as if the most important thing of all is to be known as the true self and not under any false colors. It is just this being known more sensitively and finely, in the helping process, that constitutes its difference from ordinary life experience.

To accept one's self is to realize that the human being reacts with pain and distress at the awareness of difference. One of our most cherished statements becomes our greatest delusion: much, much too soon the self ventures to say, I have learned to "accept difference." Often this is but a phase in a process, for it can also represent a plateau upon which the person remains fixed and caught in some faulty, conceptual, fabricated attitude and speech which *seems* to accept difference, when what truly occurs is a projection of a piece of the self upon the other and a resultant denial that difference exists. One cannot ever say merely that the self accepts difference and, by saying this, have understood its meaning.

Difference between the self and the other creates fear and guilt, and arouses comparisons in terms of better and worse, and reactions of thinking, "It ought to be different from what it is." We speak of a highly complicated matter, and a very slow growth, related primarily to the self, when we speak of acceptance of difference. Accepting one's own difference is something other than a matter of becoming more courageous about one's opinions. Of all things, it is least of all opinion, where one commonly thinks of it first. Neither is it a flamboyant tendency to dress bizarrely, to live unconventionally, to speak shockingly, as sometimes this "affirmation of one's own difference" is interpreted to mean; even though, too, at times the temporary expression of discovering difference comes out in these dramatic terms.

Now we come as well to the other side of "difference," also a part of the acceptance of the self: that is, an equally strong craving for likeness and unity. In fact, it is wholly suitable to bring to a close a discussion of acceptance in an effort to understand the uniting tendencies in the self, and how these tendencies lend themselves to the use of another in that special instance of the helping role. Essentially, to accept one's self as human means to accept the compelling need for relationship and the dominant role which it plays in every life. The self needs the other in order to live, in order to grow, even in order to understand itself; for it is not, as we shall see when looking at it in more detail later, a matter of understanding the self in a logical, explanatory, theoretical way. The only way one truly knows the self is through interaction with another. Feeling changes and is known only in the very act of expression. The will is felt by putting it forth and by receiving in return the impact of another will, and we seek those who give us more accurately that response. Of all the parts of the self the hardest to admit is the part that needs. To acknowledge need is to realize the existence of the source of satisfaction outside of the self, and that is a fearful admission; for the need is comprised of impulse, and the impulse feels like life itself, and therefore at times it is as if the very source of life lodges outside the self—hence out of its control, leaving it vulnerable.

This leads us finally to the admission of human limitation, limitation overwhelmingly greater than we are ever willing to admit, even in the most ordinary aspects of living. In time, in duration, in energy, in vulnerability, in control over external circumstance, we are forced to see how little control we actually have. In the process of growth, that limit which every expression of the self must somewhere encounter moves from the outside gradually into the own self. For the child, this limit, as well as the ideal, is carried by the other, usually the parents, and every human being differs with respect to this internalization of limit. Without it, there is no true freedom. But it is safe to say that no individual ever reaches the goal of feeling the limit completely within, but always needs the outside as well, in some balance that constitutes the ever-changing but ultimate reality of human psychology.

Ultimately, then, we come to this conclusion: it is the own self that the helping person must first learn to accept, and through this process he becomes better able to permit the other to be himself. This comes about not because of any exaggerated detachment, but out of the thoroughly incomprehensible phenomenon of greater capacity to relate through greater separation. More self means more wholeness within, less necessitous need on the outside, but, miraculously, richer capacity for genuine relationship.

This chapter, despite its title, has concerned itself primarily with the psychology of the helping person, and now, in the chapter which follows, but with a new focus, namely, "understanding," we arrive at a consideration of the nature of a concept constantly utilized to describe a relationship. As introductory to this further detailed examination of the same situation to which we have been devoted in these pages, it is enough to say that, when the caseworker faces the client whom he has never seen before, he does not understand him in his individuality, but understands him only in such universal terms as that he, too, is capable of some fresh acceptance of himself. The caseworker knows, as well, the partial nature of this capacity in the client, as different from his own psychological comprehension as a helping person. On account of this very difference, the caseworker feels guilt which can mislead him, unless he is willing, too, to live out this difference from the client in every word and action, without apology and without denial and without disabling guilt. For the meaning of acceptance of the self, as applied to the helping person, is not complete without the honest and courageous acceptance of the difference inherent in the responsible and powerful role which the helper has dared to assume.

CHAPTER X

THE NATURE OF UNDERSTANDING IN CASEWORK HELP

T HE WHOLE CHARACTER of the helping process changed and moved to new developmental levels when the concept of immediate response as the core of understanding came into full comprehension. From the moment of entering training in a functional setting, the student is in an experience to which this concept of the immediate response is central. It is again one of those arresting paradoxes which appear so often in psychological material that this concept, simple as it may seem, and desirable as it may appear, requires a long, slow developmental process to ensure acquiring the ability to respond that this concept holds out in promise. At the same time it can be said with equal assurance that, while this idea of fineness of response is a product and reward of deepening self-development, it is yet possible for the learner to make an immediate connection with it from the first. The beginning student experiences it in the kind of response he receives from teachers and supervisor, and, often to his surprise, he finds that in consequence he, too, is suddenly able to respond more freely and spontaneously to his clients.

There are many different kinds of understanding which the self believes it craves from the other, and all of these manifest themselves in one way or another in the helping situation. All are in a sense illusory and spurious, real as they may appear; while certainly not to be scorned, nevertheless they are only substitutes for the kind of understanding that eventually characterizes the genuine helping process.

First, there is the common understanding previously spoken of in the discussion of identification, which can only be characterized as sympathy, in which the self is met by another who seems to say to him, "How hard this has been; how much you have done; how I can feel for you!" In ordinary instances when two people begin to exchange experiences, the one telling and the other listening, it is likely to come about that the listener is suddenly reminded of a similar thing which happened to him, and as soon as he can politely do so he embarks upon a recollection of his own. It is interesting to consider what it is that passes between these two people that can be characterized as "understanding," and to realize how different it is from understanding in its functional, professional meaning. For here in the natural life situation it seems that the listener grieves with the griever, feels pain with the one who is in pain, lets fear grip him in reaction to the one possessed by fear, primarily because he himself has been through a like experience. Much of human response is of this kind, and in it experience becomes a give and take, back and forth, a discovery now of likeness, now of difference, a spinning out together of the commonplace detail of reminiscence. Here we have two people on an equal plane, relatively speaking, whose interest in each other grows out of self-centered interest in his own experience, however much this fact may be disguised. This is the exact opposite of the true helping situation, in which, as every responsible helping person soon discovers, the injection of personal stake to compare, match, or contrast the client's account with one's own experience immediately becomes an intrusion and a desertion of the client's center of interest. I recall having a supervisor tell me with that wonderful combination of delight because she now knew better, and despair that she should have made so grievous an error, that once, when her student poured out his fear of inheriting a tragic illness from a parent, she met it by admitting that she too had known a like fear. The mistake was instantly perceived through the student's instinctive rejection of this unhelpful kind of identification.

Again, there is the sense of understanding and unity between one's self and another that arises from a shared emotion, a common liking, a similar point of view, felt by both to be unique and different. Even to discover that another has felt the same way about a color or a taste or a special kind of weather adds richness and flavor to living. Yet, however beneficent and meaningful this kind of understanding, it too is not part of the structural base in a helping relationship, although it is inevitably present in one form or another. On occasion it forms the pathway by which an otherwise isolated, separated, and painfully different person begins to traverse the unknown and lets himself feel the earliest sign of uniting with an alien whole.

Yet another variety of understanding can only be described as "forgiveness," and often it seems to the helping person that it is this kind of understanding into which he falls unwittingly. The very position that he holds as helper, presupposing as it does that he possesses a key to the understanding of human dynamics, inevitably creates a pervading sense of forgiveness toward behavior which the individual himself may feel to be sinful, unworthy, and burdensome. By the act of unburdening, he rids himself of the weight and conflict momentarily, and discovers in the response of the helper that he is not as bad as he thought himself to be. To forgive is a benign and sometimes tender act, capable of a rich range, so that it is not a matter of whether it should or should not be; rather it is a matter of honesty and genuineness, in contrast to a false assumption of the right to forgive as if some Olympian source rested originally in the helper. Soon the quality of forgiveness, if it becomes a growing basis of unity between the self and the other, mounts to the point where it brings about increased denial of self-responsibility and renewed guilt feeling as a reaction to that same denial.

Very frequently the overburdened client comes with longing to be sided with against another, or against whatever the external threat or injustice is felt to be. He feels understanding in the person who agrees with him, who seems to accept exactly those arguments that he is constructing for his own justification. In this stage he depends to an agonizing degree upon external opinion, having to convince the other that he needs help and is worthy of it. Needless to say, all of this appearance of pressure in order to convince is a reflection of his mounting inner guilt, of effort to deny his own will, of unadmitted and unacknowledged fear of a new, unknown and possibly uncontrollable situation. How to contain all these strands of awareness at once: how to respond to the client's feeling that everything is against him, and yet refrain from identification with his false projection of blame upon the object—this is the great problem confronting the helping person which we are attempting to examine.

In every human self there is the universal longing at times to be understood intuitively, by a gesture, by silence, in short, by no effort of language, since language at best is always felt initially as separating rather than uniting. Indeed, this kind of momentary understanding is a blessed accompaniment of living and of relationship, provided it does not hold the self in necessitous need. For this, too, may become a negative will expression in its refusal to give any piece of the self, insisting upon being known the way one is without words. In the helping situation, but only as the fruit of developed relationship and as the product of true engagement, there are moments that are like this, informed with the sense of mystery, in the best meaning of that word. We can hold to this appreciation for the wordless connection, and yet acknowledge that only if the self can find ways to offer intrinsic pieces of its substance—only through the willing use of language, that universal means of conveying both thought and feeling—can any substantial relationship develop.

Finally, we must take cognizance of the kind of understanding which says, "You are like all others; this is natural,

is to be expected, is universal." Much response in helping is
like this and is indispensable and appropriate. Yet I have
known a person, whom I was attempting to help, tighten up,
withdraw, resist anew, in rejection of this emphasis upon likeness with all humanity, because at that very instant his own
movement was already fixed upon the affirmation of uniqueness. The emphasis upon the universal, the common, the
human, can at moments encourage the opposite of self-
responsibility, thus increasing the need for rationalization
and justification.

Now we are come at last to an effort to say more accurately
and finely what is the true nature of understanding in casework help, for important as is each one of these facets of
understanding which we have been examining, not any single
one nor yet all together serves to answer this perplexing
question satisfactorily. For now it becomes clear once more
that the problem in our use of the word understanding arises
because of the tendency to use this word always as if applied
to understanding the client, the one seeking help, whereas
its meaning can only be comprehended when permitted to
assume its rightful and inevitable focus upon understanding
the helping situation and the caseworker's own part in the
process.

Actually, the arresting fact becomes plain that in any
authentic helping process the client does not always feel
understood: on the contrary, it is impossible that he should,
since the very essence of movement originates in those
moments when he is feeling difference and separation. To
be sure, he does feel, as has already been pointed out in some
of the earlier parts of this discussion, that he is understood
in this helping situation in a way that he has never experienced before: this is different from anything he has ever
known. But it is also true that when the whole of the situation
is comprehended, that is, the completed process as it moves
from the beginning phase into ending, he also at times feels
painfully misunderstood, unaccepted the way he is, held to

an external standard which is not yet his own, especially when the helper rejects the false self in a moment of crisis.

Therefore the key to the whole problem lodges in taking hold of both sides of this psychological concept at once: the heightened, intensified sense of a kind of understanding from the helping person different from that ever before known, and the penetrating experience of being misunderstood by the same person with whom he has had such an exceptional awareness of unity. Consequently it begins to appear that the word understanding does not serve our purpose for describing the attitude of the helping person, weighted as it always is with the one-sided implication of understanding the other; perhaps, therefore, we find the key to this problem only by searching for new ways to describe what it is that does actually take place.

Stated in general terms, the nature of understanding in functional helping is comprised of an immediate awareness of the dynamics of the present moment and of the immediate situation. This awareness on the part of the helper becomes manifest in responses which grow ever more accurate and reliable with the development of the helping self. The "immediate situation" to which we refer is obviously the helping situation; the place, the time, the persons, helper and the one who seeks help, the agency, intricate and multistructured, making itself felt in every step of the process. That to which the caseworker responds, then, is the will-impulse-feeling expression of the client as it is heightened, focused, and intensified by his effort to avoid the very help he sought.

In the light of this generalization, the crucial role played by the understanding of pure psychological dynamics involved in asking for or taking help becomes paramount, and momentarily it is almost as if to say, content does not matter. The life struggle for growth can be played out on any content, whatever the client chooses. In the last analysis, whatever the content, the client is acting, thinking, feeling, under the stimulus of the helping situation which is both pressure and freedom, in a special combination of the two. The first principle the beginning helper must always learn is that which establishes the primacy of the present relationship between the helper and the one who seeks help, a relationship that will become temporarily the center of the client's life if he can finally enter into this demanding process which identifies taking help with psychological growth.

In the chapters that follow, I shall attempt to examine more finely the vital movement into engagement between two human beings in the functional helping situation, and to bring back into its appropriate place the role played by content. Both of these aspects of the problem will serve to illuminate the concept of understanding. But, first, I should like to touch once more on the related question, out of what source this kind of understanding comes to the caseworker.

It is generally accepted that the caseworker understands how to help because he has himself taken help. He has been through the same situation, not in content, but in dynamics. He knows what it is to reveal his need and to take what it requires from a source that he does not control. The danger in this generalization lies in the temptation to oversimplify by concluding that by this is meant the learning of a technique, known because experienced for one's self, and therefore in turn applied to the client. But nothing could be farther from the truth, and nothing more destructive of the true meaning of this fundamental premise. It is exactly because no technique can be learned to be applied to another, and because there are no mechanical interpretations to fall back upon, that this kind of helping process is so difficult to learn.

The understanding of the student caseworker is imbued with the heightened awareness of process: what it means to be in a process and to feel its eventuation in a time rhythm. This understanding contains the awakening realization of the universal reactions of the human self to beginnings, to change, to the pull of involvement which cannot be controlled; to ending and separation experiences. The one who is learning to help in functional terms knows, through his own process, the pull of ambivalent forces, the striving of the will, the yielding, the release of new life which is the result. All of this is at the center of understanding, and is of a wholly different order from the kind of understanding which concentrates upon interpretation of the client's behavior.

The difference which distinguishes phases of maturity in development of a professional self is a difference observable and known in terms of authenticity of response. The natural self tends to project its own experience and assumes its truth for everyone. In this phase there is little separation between self and not-self, the latter being largely colored and shaped by internal need, so that the world becomes a part of the self as whole.

True, in a later phase of development—in any phase which is a product of inner growth—the self also must continue to project its own experience, but now this experience is more reliably universal, more aware, less the victim of illusion and denial. It is in order to live up to this demand of universality, to respond accurately, that the inner experience must be informed with precision, candor, and authenticity, which is the same as saying it must be lived truly and honestly. This is the core of the meaning of understanding.

CHAPTER XI

THE SIGNIFICANCE OF THE
IMMEDIATE PRESENT

Among all the concepts of which functional casework makes
use, none is so difficult to understand, so hard to learn
in actual doing, so elusive of precise definition, as the meaning of the immediate present in the helping situation. In fact,
there is no other way about it than to admit at the ouset this
limitation: that its meaning will defy those who search for it
analytically. Only by a kind of yielding to the nature of the
material with which we work: mobile, dynamic, fluid with
the very stuff of life itself, understood momentarily and lost
again, by its very motion incapable of being arrested long
enough to become conceptual, can we hope to find whatever
of understanding is possible. It is worth saying once again
that the development of the professional self is marked by
just this kind of willingness to understand in new ways—a
willingness which asks as well the relinquishment of the
search for unchanging assurance in a world comprised of
change.

All that we have attempted to examine here as characteristic
of the disciplined helper—identification, acceptance, engagement, understanding, and response—is so much preliminary
exploration to bring us at last to this consideration of what
actually occurs in the immediate present of the helping situation. For now we come face to face with the exacting
demands upon the strength contained within the helper, and
are ready to ask, to what purpose, to what use, to what end?
To the purpose, we have said, that another human being
may gain, through the use of the helper, more self, more life,

and hence more capacity to cope with inner and outer reality.

This is a new kind of strength of which we strive to speak and to the learning of which we devote ourselves. I have spoken in a previous chapter of the striving toward fuller use of the capacity of the self as the only satisfying explanation to account for the motivation which brings any person into the helping role. Yet it is a very different kind of creativity from that to which we are accustomed, and in its very difference lies its unique character. Creativity, in its more natural expression, goes out to work change upon material, to effect through the material the image of the own idea, the own inner truth. The self pushes outward compellingly upon what is, with ongoing unity of will and impulse and emotion —whole, powerful, and expanded with spirit. It creates upon the material, to effect its change. It is the self projected, enlarged because it makes, shapes, and fashions, feels its strength, and is alive on account of it. For the helper, the situation seems just the reverse: what is required is the capacity to permit the other to create upon the self, and this is hardly a lesser thing but even an expansion of comprehending what creativity can be.

In this hour the helping person lives wholly on behalf of another's need, and that is indeed a very great deal to ask. It is perhaps one reason why this role comes more naturally to the woman than to the man, for characteristically the masculine will goes out upon the object with power, strength, intent, and direction. The woman by nature is more attuned to containment and lends herself more readily to the giving over of the whole self to the use of another. The biologically creative role is like this, for in the nine months of the uterine experience the whole focus of the organism changes to the nurture of the new being which takes from the fertile ground in which it is planted. It is this lending of the self to the use of another which must be comprehended: the organic sensitivity of a whole, big enough to contain, like the support of earth itself, capable of love and tenderness as well as unyielding difference.

It is this lending of the self to the use of another which is the first thing to be felt and known in learning to help. And, strangely enough, it is a very different thing from humility or depreciation of self, or overvaluation of the other. It comes about only through the full awareness and valuing of one's own self, through accepting the strength and becoming responsible for it. That this strength is needed to the utmost in any process of helping is what becomes gradually and then ever more compellingly realized as experience in helping matures.

There are many ways of describing for what purpose the helping person needs to be possessed of strength of unusual quality and depth. But each partial explanation or illustration serves only to becloud the one ultimate fact about the process of helping, and if this is first stated, looked upon with fresh eyes, examined, then every other facet of what transpires can be understood in relation to this central core.

The gist of the matter is that, in every helping process where something does indeed take place, there comes a time when all the strength of the client is gathered into one mighty effort to overcome the strength of the helping person; and if he succeeds, his movement is defeated, and if he does not succeed, he may have won new life. From that time on the process moves to new levels. This moment happens not rarely but abundantly. It is an inexplicable moment, and yet its outlines are sharp and vivid. It is the use of the self in this moment that the helping person strives to learn, and in comparison every other demand for response pales into relative unimportance. For now the demand upon the helping person is to hold steady and firm and unshakable against a powerful onslaught masked and disguised in content that can be very misleading.

It is not difficult to understand why the helping person

should find it so hard to meet this moment and to respond with discrimination and precision; the wonder is that it is learned at all, and that it can be borne, considering the combination of spontaneity and accuracy, feeling and strength, courage and doubt which so often resides in it. The doubt that besets the helping person and interferes with the full use of the self in this moment springs from the fact that this maintenance of the own strength, in the face of external effort to overcome it, is in itself a powerful will expression, and, as such, is imbued with guilt, as any expression of the human will inevitably is. Furthermore, one cannot maintain this kind of strength helpfully unless the feeling for the other person remains devoted to his life's movement, and includes and values the intrinsic genuine self. At bottom, the impact upon the client of this moment is the impact of knowing that even this expression of himself is valued, and to be valued really for what one is, is the most important thing, as he soon discovers.

To give an immediate response in a helping process puts upon the caseworker the responsibility for the awareness of that moment when the powerful will of the client is gathered into a focus to pit itself against the external strength, now felt to reside in the helper. Through some strange fact of being, yet not so strange, it is the essence of growth that the too-powerful, too-negative, too-resistive will, which craves to force the outer reality to yield to its need, must now instead yield itself to the greater strength outside its own singleness. At one and the same time, the person seeking help mobilizes every shred of available power to conquer the greater strength on the outside; but his greatest need is to meet, feel, and yield to a strength greater than his own. Every person can know this great need which lies at the bottom of all human experience, both in natural relationship and in functional relationship, and can realize as well, at least in some partial way, the burden and weight of carrying that strength internally; in a word, becoming responsible for it.

We use the word yielding, with purpose to characterize this moment in time, and in its use know what depths of doubt and reservation can be stirred by this word which implies surrender, hence defeat. Yet when one comes to terms with its reality, the reward is a deepening comprehension of the dynamics of this change-imbued moment. The flood of emotion which frees the constricted will carries the movement into new and deeper levels.

What actually seems to occur is the making of that fundamental choice toward growth which is the crisis in the process. The negative organization of the will that has held the self in bondage breaks up, and emotion is fresh and real. Need— internal psychic need—heretofore feared and denied, is known, realized, possessed. The self rests, momentarily, in the support of a strength not its own. The emotion is peace after battle. The impulse which breaks through releasingly is suddenly the conveyor of energy and spontaneity. In this receptive, vulnerable, feeling phase, the new element which is other-than-self can be received instead of refused, and to that new element, in whatever content it takes form, the old self must find a new relation. This holds the key to all development of relationship to the outside world. It signalizes the capacity for and the realization of a constructive utilization of the inevitable. This is neither adjustment (which requires bending the self to conform to an outer mold) nor compromise (which suggests abandonment of a part of the true self). It is evidence of the creative power of the psychic energies in the self; hence, growth.

By the measure of his capacity to utilize this process the client also discovers new capacity to find relation to the others in his personal life experience. At bottom this has been his problem when he comes to the social agency, whatever form the outer reality may have assumed. The self is not whole without the capacity to relate to the other, and finding relation to the other means discovery that the other, too, has powerful will and impulse energies, which interact with his own, and which he cannot control. If he is to live at all, then he must find the way to accept this inevitable fact.

The immediate present is imbued with fear because it, more than the past or the future, contains the fear of living. It is this responsibility for living which the human self perversely tries to avoid at the same time that he craves it so compellingly. It is not a matter of getting rid of this fear, which in every instance is impossible, but wholly a matter of finding the way to live with the fear in such a way as to make life bearable; more than this, to turn the fear to creative use. In the unusual sense of unity which at times is felt in the helping situation, it is as if the fear diminishes or is at least momentarily supported in a whole larger than the own self. Having discovered that one can unite without being destroyed, one knows anew that the capacity to unite holds great promise for life. Within this unity, so dearly prized and newly won, comes the inevitable separation which this precipitating moment of difference has introduced. Now he is faced, not with the fear of unity, but more with the fear of separation: the isolated, single, separated sense of the own self, alone and unconnected with the supporting whole. To traverse this lack of connection, to recreate it, to find his way back toward the relationship with another is the crisis he cannot escape. His forward movement toward it is growth, no less. Upon the helping person rests the necessity to know and respond to that forward movement.

The desire of one who writes of this, as of the person who reads, must indeed be to find some way to convey in concrete, visual illustration the tangible evidence of how this pure psychological movement lives itself out in everyday experience. Somehow it seems impossible to convey at one and the same time the dynamics of the engagement between the helper and the one seeking help, and the specific content in which this engagement occurs. For that reason I have chosen to devote one chapter to a discussion of the meaning of content and its relation to psychological change.

It now seems possible to lay the groundwork for a further generalization regarding content. We have stripped the meaning of immediate response of all but the clear, sharp focus of response to the expression of the will-impulse-feeling strivings of the client. We have attempted first to comprehend the dynamic of pure psychological movement which grows out of the awareness of the crisis and the movement that follows yielding. If the response of the helper is to content as a sheer matter of content, the helping potential is lost. Yet content holds an all-important place, for none of this is possible without the projection of the inner conflict upon outer, partialized bits of reality. And it is the character of this reality, the structural nature of the process, which now remains to be explored.

CHAPTER XII

THE RELATION OF CONTENT TO PSYCHOLOGICAL CHANGE

THERE COMES a moment in the training process when swift forward movement results from the sudden realization on the part of the student that it does not matter so much what one says, as that one becomes genuinely engaged with the client. To react spontaneously, to throw off the constricting intellectual bonds of necessity to find the right thing to say, is like discovering a whole new medium in which to work. The moment of this discovery is enlivening and usually comes about, if it happens at all, through some sudden illumination, never by a slow, laborious accretion of learning. It is the moment of recognition that the very helping situation itself is the crucial matter, and that whatever of therapeutic value is possible for the client resides in this new experience with a helping person who assists him toward self-understanding and a new capacity to will constructively. As one student put it in writing a final casework paper, "As we ponder we lose the moment and then it is too late; once we ponder, the emotion is gone and with it the feeling and the spontaneity."

Every helping person will bear testimony to this actual experience, that the best results are obtained and the most enlivening sense of engagement and movement is present "when there is no time to think." In these moments there is a realization of rhythm, of wholeness within the helping person, of willingness to risk, of freedom from caution—in a word, of courageous giving of the self to a process on behalf of another. From this exhilarating generalization it might be easy to jump to the conclusion that all that is required is absence of restraint, whereas the kind of spontaneity of which we speak is, as this whole discussion has tried to indicate, the product of a long, slow growth of internal discipline which produces just this freedom to use the self spontaneously in the functional situation as it unfolds.

We speak here of that same relation of form to creativity which is the essence of any discipline. Content in the helping process bears the same relation to psychological change as form to creativity: content is the form in which inner experience communicates itself. In ordinary experience we feel emotion about something; if we are afraid, we are afraid because of something; if we feel guilty, we locate the cause of the guilt upon a specific act or thought. Inner and outer, abstract and concrete, the psychic life and content are inseparable parts of a whole, two sides of the same phenomenon. It is only through the medium of content that there can be development in relationship, while at bottom the content corresponds exactly to pure psychological interaction between two human wills. I stress the area of ordinary experience because content plays precisely this crucial role in all human interaction, including the functional helping situation, yet at the same time it is essential to keep in mind that, as the discipline in the helping role grows and deepens, there comes about a corresponding enrichment of the helper's capacity to work with pure psychological movement and emotion almost without content. There comes as well a maturing realization that the fundamental emotions of fear and guilt are inherent in the life process itself, needing no justification or explanation in terms of external events. The possession of this knowledge constitutes one of the major differences between the helper and the one being helped, inasmuch as the latter seeks always to justify or explain in real terms.

It will readily be seen how this realization of the importance of pure psychological dynamics between two human beings in different roles, almost to the exclusion of content, is an indispensable phase in the process of learning to become a helper. In fact it can be said that, unless the student is capable of an exaggerated abandonment of content, he never wholly succeeds in throwing off the bondage to the reality content that is the natural characteristic of the beginner. He must learn to regard the will-impulse-feeling interaction between caseworker and client as the essence of the authentic helping situation. But in the process of establishing this concept the true significance and value of content may be overlooked, and, if this is so, then one important facet of the total situation is left obscure and inaccessible. It remains to ask, what is the significance of content; what relation does it bear to psychological change?

There are two key points in this problem of content which can guide the caseworker in dealing with its diverse detail. The first lies in the principle that the response of the caseworker must be not to content as such, but to the will-impulse-feeling expression of the self in relationship. In the functional helping situation, one side of the relationship is the client; the other side, the caseworker—agency-centered—who now constitutes for the client otherness, non-self, the external object upon which the client can project his conflict and his dynamic pattern of use of self in relationship. Accuracy of response in the caseworker lies in feeling sensitively what is projected upon and done to him as the helper, and this can be expressed in an infinite variety of content.

The second key point lies in the realization that the very uniqueness of casework arises from the discovery of the value for therapeutic results which comes about through devoted consideration for, and use of, content. The constant penetration of reality factors existing both in the client's situation and in the agency's function is the most meaningful factor for differentiating casework from therapy. The distinctive character of function in casework arises from this utilization of the potential for growth through the reworking of a concrete, partialized, limited, specific content within a process especially established in structure for this purpose. Parenthetically, it might be added that this same thing is true in the learning-teaching experience within the functional setting provided for casework training; namely, that, by a close adherence to all facets of the purpose that brings the student into training, therapeutic results are possible. As has been stated earlier, there is fear of this use of the word therapeutic, in part because the solid ground of function seems momentarily lost in confusion of casework with therapy. Yet one of the essential differences between the two, from the point of view of the process, lies in this important and significant area of the use of content.

For the caseworker, there are three identifiable phases of development in relation to this problem of the use of content. The first is characterized by an exaggerated attention to content. This is the natural attitude which the student first brings into training, and it is wholly logical, for, if one is to help with a reality problem, then what is more reasonable than that both the helper and the one being helped should focus wholly upon solving this problem. Let us say that in this phase content holds the center of the stage. Supervisors will recognize this phase as analogous to their own experience in learning to supervise, when their attention is concentrated upon the case, to the detriment of the worker's learning.

The second phase of learning is the one I speak of at the opening of this chapter, namely, the sudden awakening to the value of spontaneity in the helping situation. This is a moment of illumination, of newly acquired freedom, and often of some very much enlivened capacity to help. A quality comes into the interview which has been altogether lacking before.

In the third and final phase the helping person has taken full possession of the dynamics of psychological movement and the meaning of the current experience in the helping milieu, at the same time that he possesses a sensitive capacity to work in the medium of the content which is natural to the client.

Such schematization of phases is useful and meaningful only if viewed as a fluid and constantly shifting relation of parts to the whole. For this sequence of events could as well describe the continuous development of the experienced helper, reflecting as it does the constant swings and advances and retreats which make up the search for greater skill so long as this search is alive. There is no better way to highlight this very point than by reference again to that most meaningful statement of Rank's informed with new meaning for casework by Miss Robinson's quotation of it in *A Changing Psychology:* ". . . One must learn the speech of the other, and not force upon him the current idiom."[1] In this lies every facet of the meaning of content for which we search. In fuller context, Rank points out the relation of the universal and individual factors which correspond to the two sides of this phenomenon: ". . . The essential factor remains always the capacity to understand the individual from himself, in which process the common human element, certainly not to be denied, can constitute only the hypothesis, not the content of the understanding."[2]

This "capacity to understand the individual from himself" means a capacity to relate creatively to the content of the experience, as the individual himself fashions it, for this is the intrinsic essence of his uniqueness; it is the individual expression of the "I," and the generalization, so important to casework, of "respect for the individual" demands this utmost respect for the content, for the reality situation, the way the client sees it and works upon it. It is in this medium that he can create to the extent of which he is capable.

It is by no means an easy matter to differentiate between these two possible and contrasting attitudes toward content, the one attitude being a sensitive response to the client's individuality, the other attitude being the excessive and unsuitable concentration upon content which always interferes with effective helping. When the helping person becomes too centered in concern for the concrete reality problem which the client brings, a number of different results are bound to occur in one way or another in the course of events. When the helping person reaches out and touches the concrete reality problem, by suggestion, advice, excessive or inappropriate concern, then the immediate effect is likely to be that the client discovers the very channel for unburdening the weight of his problem: something he seeks but which will defeat him in the end if he is successful. Reference has already been made in this discussion to the universal tendency, on the part of the one who comes for help, to come with necessity to blame other persons, or to blame events over which he has no control, or circumstances which have victimized him, as the cause of his tribulations. He believes that change means change of the outside. He does not yet know, and cannot, that it is only through change within himself that he can achieve his desired goal; that he alone can do it. Readily the connection between the two attitudes is evident: the connection between the caseworker's over-concern for the reality problem and the client's desire to be rid of the burden. The problem becomes the caseworker's, and over and over again one sees a whole process continue indefinitely, with just this struggle unresolved.

The same struggle comes about when the helping person reaches out and takes hold of the concrete problem through some mistaken effort to share with the client the burden of solution of the reality problem. The reality situations of finding a job, or consulting a physician, or finding a place to live are particularly full of risk with respect to this undesirable result. One can hardly believe that the human self can for so long hold itself in bondage to the continuous need to force the other, the helping person, to carry this pack upon his back, when inherently he will fight every move which seems to indicate that his efforts have succeeded.

Here we have before us a valuable opportunity to see and

consider the relation between content and psychological change. We have spoken again and again, in different connections, of the one fundamental movement which takes place when the user of help takes over into himself both the problem and the responsibility for its solution. I use the figure of speech "pack on the back" advisedly, because it seems to me at times one can almost feel this in kinesthetic terms, and can know the moment this shift takes place from one's self, who holds the will-to-growth, to the one using help, who now takes it over. Unfortunately this does not stay put as simply as the carrying of a load, but moves again constantly back and forth. So that here the question, will he himself take this responsibility for this particular content, carries the full meaning of the imperative psychological change which must come about, if he is to use himself differently.

Likewise, the over-concentration of attention upon the content by the helping person soon shapes up to become the bone of contention over which the will-struggle eventuates. For now it becomes still more clear that if the helping situation ever runs into those rocky waters where but one goal is in sight, and this the goal of the helping person, then, indeed, the client, often to his own great disadvantage, will set his will against it. He opposes seldom, if ever, in the clear-cut discernible manner of open refusal of the plan of the caseworker, where it could certainly be got hold of, but more often in the subtler ways of resistance (characteristic of mankind, not evil in the client). He may appear to be in complete agreement with the caseworker, he may be making devoted efforts to achieve the goal, but with striking lack of success. "I will do what you want," he will say in complete submission and conformity. "If I can only find out exactly what you are asking of me, I assure you I will do it," he adds. Or, even more frustrating to the helper, the client acts precisely in accordance with what was agreed upon between them, and promptly the most undesirable consequences ensue from his praiseworthy efforts.

In other words, it is the content which eventually distills the situation into the pure form of the clash of two wills. It is for this reason that the use of a worker-conceived plan is imbued from the outset with the seeds of its own defeat.

So far it seems relatively simple to follow the course of this exploration, but now we come to more complex and more illusive phenomena. It would be an easy reaction to what has just been said to abandon altogether our interest in the reality problem which the client brings, lest any of these results be produced; lest, when the caseworker touches the problem, it cease to be the client's. Yet we have also said that it is of the essence of functional casework that there should be felt and expressed, throughout the process, utter regard and consideration for the content the client brings. "Getting at the feeling which lies back of his words"; "waiting for the relationship to develop in order that he may feel sufficiently at ease to reveal his true feelings"; "knowing that what he says when he first comes is not the true meaning, but eventually the true meaning will come forth"—all of these expressions which appear in casework literature are wholly alien to and destructive of the meaning we are attempting to examine. Actually every word the client speaks, from first to last, is important to him, of genuine meaning, hence to be valued and given consideration as a part of himself. If he has made a plan, as he so often has when he first comes to the agency, just because he must so desperately feel that he is not so badly off as he may appear to be, it is worthy of every attention from the caseworker. Out of their actual working together upon this problem and plan as he brings it will come the testing of what he has created; the caseworker need be in no haste to inject his own doubt.

I have spoken in the previous chapter of the crisis which originates, and which is present in every process, when the one being helped gathers all his strength into one focus and attempts to overcome the greater strength of the helping person. And I have said that if that outer strength holds he may possibly win new life, and if it succumbs the process fails. Now we are ready to develop in more detail what the nature of that engagement can be and often is, because the erroneous conclusion could be reached that this encounter of one strength with another is always a matter of two opposing judgments or opinions, of which that of the caseworker must prevail. Rarely is it this, although sometimes it may be; but if it is, then the clash of wills likely to occur is of that kind which, no matter what the outcome, results in the failure of the client to receive help. In fact, the very nature of the strength in the helping person may be evident not from his insistence upon a single outcome but rather in continuous capacity to make no issue of what the final outcome may be.

This is but a particular instance of the fundamental principle which can now be restated. In any process, the psychological dynamics are the same—they represent the universal, the common, the like, that which is always the same wherever authentic involvement in the giving and taking of help occurs. Content, on the other hand, represents that which is individual, unique, different. In consequence, the relation of content to psychological change becomes comprehensible only as the helper can leave behind the necessity to interpret content in mechanistic terms and respond to it instead as the conveyor of the real self, dynamically lived out in the present.

Any process will show universal points of crisis in psychological movement, but always through content which is unique. Perhaps we can understand the whole problem of the generic and specific in casework through this very point: what it takes, for instance, for a caseworker to move from one specific function to another. About this we believe two seemingly contradictory things: one, that there is a common base which is the same for every function; the other, that it is just the difference in the function itself which provides an indispensable ingredient in effective helping. The contradiction is resolved in the belief that the helping person must possess and carry from one function to another this deep level of understanding of psychological movement, which has the same essential outlines of movement in every process. At the same time it is the content, which is the form, the individualization of the function, which must be learned anew, and the learning of which requires a process of internalization in time.

There will be content in every process that reflects the tentativeness of the beginning movement, compounded as it is of wanting and not wanting at the same time. There will be the gathering toward the center of the first crisis, when the one seeking help tests his own strength against the helping person, feels the greater strength on the outside, halts ambivalently, struggles, then yields to it, and from it discovers he gains a new release toward forward movement. Then follows a new beginning, this time initiating the longer sweep of the continuing process, repeating again upon another level the ambivalence and tentativeness, the building toward a crisis, the crisis, the yielding, the new movement forward. Until at last comes ending, and at the crisis of ending, which represents more than any other point the imposition of an immovable limit, the whole activation of the will conflict poses once more the touch-and-go: will he, or will he not, take over his own growth movement?

For each of these points of crisis, and for each of the slower gradual sweeps of movement in the process, there is content suitable to the function and self-created by the client. It is with content that he creates. The fixed, unchangeable nature of his psychological make-up as a human being he cannot escape, and the agency structure in the helping situation precisely reflects this life reality; but in the medium of his own content he can create to the utmost of his capacity.

What the helping person feels, as he relates to the particular individual content of the one seeking help, is the effect of the will-impulse-feeling strivings as they become more intense, more sharply etched in outline, under the unusual circumstance of the functional helping situation. What he feels is movement toward the source of help, or movement away; effort to elicit emotion from the helper; effort to control his own; drive to exaggerate helplessness, or painful acknowledgment of need. He feels the will in all its force manifestations: to change the day, the time, the conditions; to change whatever it is the helping person has set up, no matter what its nature. He begins to feel the searching, the testing, the effort to discover: can the helping person really take me as I am? Will what I am shock, frighten, alienate this one who attempts to help? To understand this, one must recapitulate still another concept, namely, that the craving of the self to be understood is never satisfied by understanding of the good side alone. In some compelling manner, the striving of the self is toward a goal that the other regard him honestly, essentially in his essence. It does not matter, then, whether it is valued good or bad, generous or mean, big or petty, honest or calculating. The self wants to be known for itself, real, exact, accurate, genuine, honestly conceived. And when it happens between two people that some approximation of this utterly unachievable goal is reached, it is a moment of rare human experience indeed. Thus, when the one using help has first felt this sense of "he accepts me the way I am," he will keep on trying to discover whether this is indeed really the case—will it hold. He will go on producing more and more content by which to further this intention. For this purpose, content is truly inexhaustible. The will of the client is bent upon discovering where there is a weak spot, and if it can be found he will go through it—perversely, to be sure, for what he requires above all else (if the life impulse has any strength) is that he should not succeed in this endeavor. To this outer strength he craves to yield the too-tight organization of himself, but this does not happen until he has pitted his own will and yielded in the process.

With children, the use of content in this manner is much plainer than with adults, and to anyone attuned to these dynamics the fact is inescapable that the child seeks always to discover what will stop him, where that outer limit is, and whether the adult really means what he says. The content which children use, and especially that which adolescents use, is swift, directly inspired by the relation to the helper, much nearer the surface and uncomplicated by rationalization. It propels itself outward straight as an arrow upon the caseworker, with an arrow's intent to attack. This is one reason, if not the key reason, why it is so difficult to work with a child in the helping process, and why a child in the way he senses an adult's relation to him can be frightening in his immediate awareness. The caseworker can give sorely needed help to a foster parent on just this score, because a child will move from home to home, getting the better of every adult, until he encounters one strong enough to meet his strength with greater strength. One must distinguish, when speaking of this point of crisis, between the adult who opposes the will of the child out of fear that the child will get the better of him, and the adult whose action arises from a source essentially tender, and internally imbued with strength. At bottom, this is the core of the problem of the delinquent; and the source of help lies in his finding the combination of a strength which says, "this cannot be," at the same time that it is related to him compassionately.

Sometimes the use of content by the client is designed to enlist the caseworker as an ally against an unjust fate. He pictures himself as the helpless victim of circumstance—one who cannot be blamed, because what has happened has happened, and the odds against him have been too great. Any process which remains on this level becomes static. For as surely as content of this character appears, there is bound to be the equally compelling drive to be found responsible, reprehensible as the end result may be. At times the client will be insisting that he did this, caused this to happen, is responsible, when the caseworker is still sympathizing with him in his fate. Movement will come, life will be affirmed, help will be used, when the caseworker recognizes and responds to the self-responsibility which he affirms. For his need to establish this responsibility accurately can be understood only when placed side by side with the acknowledgment that, until he feels responsibility for what has been happening and is happening, he cannot mobilize his strength to encounter outer reality successfully.

The relation of past to present is of especial interest when examined from the particular focus of attempting to comprehend the relation of content to psychological change. Content from the past is unquestionably utilized repeatedly as a means by which to force the process out of the present into the past, where there is less fear. Content from the past can carry the full sweep of the overassertion of projected blame: what I am is because of what happened to me in the past; what my childhood lacked or had too much of; what others did or failed to do. Hence the past becomes a vital strand in disentangling self-responsibility, own will, admission of own will, from the projection upon others.

In the content of the past is located the stream of continuity of the self, both in individuality and in ancestry. The past gives expanse and enlargement to the self; one cannot be whole unless one possesses one's past, encompassing it lovingly whatever its content, for the very reason that it is a part of one's self. The process of growth seems to demand that in some manner the self rework a crisis in experience which lodges like an unassimilated weight on account of excessive guilt, or denied responsibility, or any other kind of denial which hides the real truth from the inner self. As I have witnessed again and again this process of growth which comes through the utilization of a piece of content from the past, it seems to be that what occurs is a sudden fresh sense of self and life arising as a result of the dropping away of the denial; a sudden realization of one's own expression of will. At the same time, the true emotion belonging to the past situation is felt genuinely, and this is possible exactly on account of the present experience in a growth process.

Content from the past tends always to be especially concerned with the relation of the self to the parents. Some schools of therapeutic psychology locate their search for cure upon the illumination of these early relations of child to parent, and formulate their solutions in causal explanation. This is vastly different from the concept here being developed. Here we are saying that, indeed, these early parental relations have been the milieu in which the child has grown. But it is because the parents represent the first objects of outer will—the crucial "otherness" of the child's life—that these relationships play so vital a role. Here the whole dynamic interplay of the pattern of self, consisting of psychological and physical need, of effort to satisfy that need, of willingness to admit the need, of will and the denial of will, of capacity to feel emotion, is played out in growth of the self. What the helper can know in the immediate moment of the helping situation is that this same dynamic pattern of the self, modified by the passage of time, by growth or lack of it, but especially by the impact of the current situation, will once more express itself authentically, and the outline of the pattern will be more precise, the more accurate the response of the helper and the richer the sense of life in the current process is.

Sometimes, in the process, the person using help comes to the threshold of comprehending this connection between past and present. He will say he knows that he must oppose the helper because he repeats the experience of the past when he opposed the imposition of his father's authority. But what he feels and actually responds to *is* the authority of the helper in the present moment—an authority which comes from the very fact of presuming to be one who can help; which comes from every reality factor in the helping situation, no matter how gentle the helper may be. It is only a question: will this be denied; will it be overasserted; or will it be acknowledged and utilized constructively?

Hence it is not that the one seeking help repeats an old experience out of need to return to the past. It is that the dynamic pattern of the self is actually and intensely alive at the moment, but in the content of the past it is more possible to communicate this fact with less fear, less guilt, less demand for being responsible in the present moment. This view of the relation of past content to the present places no requirement upon the one in the growth experience to use any particular piece of content, nor does a wealth of content have to be reworked in this manner. Any piece of content can convey the same dynamic movement, and the individuality of the self in the present is epitomized in this very selection of content and in the location of the vortex in which the life movement eventuates.

The more the content moves from past to present, the more likelihood there is of fear arising, and this is as true for the helper as for the one seeking help. It is that crisis which, of all points of crisis, asks the maximum in strength of the helper. A great variety of content presents itself in this especial moment, since it is the moment during which the one seeking help opens the innermost recesses of the self and puts into words the specific, the fact, upon which he locates his deepest fear. Since no human being, even the one who has disciplined himself to be a helper, is ever completely free of fear and guilt in the life process, this moment can become a true crisis, for the entanglement in another's fear is an eventuality to which live creatures are peculiarly susceptible. On exactly this point the disciplined helper differs from the one seeking help, for the essence of authentic growth is a constant change in which the self finds new relation to fear and increasing capacity to differentiate himself with respect to this emotion. This is a highly complex psychological phenomenon, and one which can scarcely be touched in so brief a manner, but neither would the subject of content be complete without inclusion of this point of major importance.

In bringing this chapter to a conclusion, there remains but one more point with respect to content which cannot be overlooked. I refer to the difference which exists between the caseworker's content and that of the client, a difference more often obliterated than acknowledged. The client is in every sense of the word a "lay" person, and thus much closer in ideology, values, prejudices, trusts, and distrusts to the general public than to the social worker. At times, social work tends to erase this fact by assuming likeness between itself and the client and difference between itself and the public. Actually, any semblance of likeness between social worker and client in content terms is projection. Likeness, which is essential in order to help, arises instead from the universals of human experience.

Agency content is created, by and large, by social workers, with respect to time, method, standards, money, and general outlook upon life. At the same time, the statement is validly made that the structure of a social agency must represent a segment of reality, a partial experience, in order to afford an effective setting for helping. A moment's thought will soon illuminate the startling and surprising character of the content a client meets when he comes to a social agency.

Content of infinite variety is implicit in what the agency stands for, in what the worker represents. The client will react to this content, if he is helped to reach these reactions. It is a content which, among other things, stands for change, growth, and life, and the potential for its realization. It is a content which, while seemingly unencumbered by a specific norm demanding a specific kind of life content, does nevertheless stand for a value whose attainment is cherished and whose realization is the hardest demand upon the human self. This is the demand—in the last analysis self-imposed—which asks that the self become responsible and carry its part in relationship with integrity and increasing willingness to trust itself to the life process.

If one accepts this conception of the relation of content to dynamics, then there is but one conclusion regarding reliance on the meaning of any particular piece of content: there can never be any one interpretation, and content out of process is practically meaningless. What may at one point of time, place, and process be a true indication of yielding, may at another be only another step into the dark helplessness of the client's fixed resistance. What may in one situation be evidence of increasing capacity for relationship, may in another be an equally powerful indication of absence of relationship. Knowing this, caseworkers can see how they could not, and should not, arrive at prior decisions before a process begins. What the caseworker can know reliably is what this human being does in the actuality of agency setting; whether he is capable of relating, is relatively responsible, reachable, accessible to communication. Even though this principle with respect to the necessity of process is acknowledged, efforts still persist in the direction of attempting to make a prior decision out of process, regarding the nature, extent, and degree of seriousness of the client's problem, in order to determine what kind of help he needs.

CHAPTER XIII

THE MOVEMENT OF THE SELF
IN CHOICE

I T BECOMES increasingly clear, as we follow step by step the exploration of these concepts in which functional helping is rooted, that we are dealing here with a process in which the client is helped to become free to choose, and that he does not bring this condition of freedom into the helping situation in any accessible or active form. Clear as this statement may seem, and however universal the agreement that helping aims toward precisely this end, of releasing capacity for choice, the reverse attitude prevails in both thought and action. At times caseworkers fall victim to an illusion to which mankind is peculiarly susceptible: that freedom is a natural state of being which will prevail so long as nothing interferes and provided the environment is favorably inclined toward its encouragement. We speak of leaving the client free to choose, of allowing him to discover his own way, of protecting his right to self-determination, without realizing the extent to which each of these descriptions of the condition of relationship between helper and helped is static and negative in the sense that each implies refraining from interference, rather than the active engagement which the helping process requires.

Accordingly, in order to comprehend the true nature of the movement of the self in choice, we must first open up and consider the more authentic realities of freedom, in terms of inner experience, psychologically explored. Interestingly enough, the words freedom and choice always go together in some intrinsic compatibility, since the state of inner being which we comprehend as freedom leads always to the enlarged capacity to choose; in a word, to affirm the will constructively, to know what one wants, and to seek it effectively. The exploration of this problem has led us to the inescapable conclusion that inner psychic freedom is a state of being, achieved only through long and arduous and painful life experience. It is the product of growth and individuation and, even under the best of circumstances, is never wholly possessed. The most we can ever hope for is some partial realization of the answer to this longing to be free. In the helping process what takes place can never be more than the most limited, temporary, and unpretentious striving for new freedom; but this in no way demeans the goal, for the search gains new vitality out of the very admission of its partial nature, and sets in motion a growth process whose on-going impulse will continue to seek out new development.

This is the fundamental truth which every helping person must at bottom admit and accept, first for the own self, in order to hold it in constant relation to the helping process. It is precisely the fact that the client lacks freedom to choose and act which brings him to the source of help, and it is his location of the responsibility for this absence of freedom upon the outside which keeps him from realizing the degree to which he can be an effective force to free himself.

But to a degree far greater than we are usually willing to admit, and to an extent that we are fearful to concede, the crisis in the helping process is more truthfully described as a process of helping the client achieve a new relation to the *inevitable,* instead of uncovering constantly new sources of choice. Through a state of affairs seen at times only as thoroughly contradictory and illogical, through this very acceptance of the inevitable, through admission of what cannot be different, of what will not succumb to the own will or force, the human self finds new life, new constructive use of himself. We speak in no sense of a fatalistic submission to what is, in hopelessness and despair, but we speak instead of the unquenchable life-force of the human spirit to grapple with outer circumstances anew.

From the moment of birth man experiences the first overpowering reality of the fixed nature of his environment. That he is born at all, in this moment of time rather than any other, of these parents; that he is endowed with a given physical constitution in sex, color, and appearance; that he is destined to play his part in an already existing environment—all these are reality factors which allow him little if any opportunity for his own choice. He shares in common with all humanity the attributes of being human, of a finite life, of the necessity to struggle in order to live at all, of a nature ambivalent with life and non-life, veined with fear and guilt, and impelled forward by a compelling search to complete himself. All his life, if he can but bear to admit it, he struggles with and against the unchangeable nature of the inner and outer reality, always with unpredictable but potentially creative results. In the span of a life's history he encounters and grapples with innumerable important occasions for choices. First these decisions are made for him by adults, such as where he shall live, what he shall wear and eat, to what school he shall go; later he takes these on himself as he moves into the crucial life decisions of an occupation, of relationship to the other, of movement from place to place, of creating a home, and somewhere, in some far less tangible way, the choice of the way and the depth of the fulfillment of the self. Indeed, the nature of the choice with which he is faced at these points of crisis is deep and complicated and sometimes overpowering in realization of the responsibility which the self cannot escape. In outer appearance, it is the multiplicity of choice and the burden of too much choice, rather than its limitation, which is more predominantly apparent. But beneath it all lies the first comprehensive life reality of the nature and extent of the limitation arising simultaneously from external environment and innate capacity of the self.

One can understand the meaning of this inevitability only by searching the everyday experience of one's own reality. On behalf of the client, we are likely to realize as well how much greater and more powerful are the odds against him, even if viewed in purely economic terms. This we need to realize and include within our thinking, but not to the exclusion of the fact which lies at a deeper level: that no matter how plentiful the reality choices appear to be in the helping situation, every client, and every person in the dynamics of the helping movement whatever the function, is finally and at last faced with the one, single, ultimate choice, will he choose growth or will he refuse it. In this moment of choice, its character is not imbued with variety—it is tight with singleness. He has sorted and sifted to this one point of impact, where the conditions of the helping situation and the character of the helper, upon whom he has located all manner of projections, constitute now the unchangeable, the inevitable; and the only question which remains becomes the same one of which we have already spoken—can he take in what is, permit the resultant disorganization of the status quo of the self, and through this means cross the threshold to the richer possibilities which await him. This is the precise moment of likeness between the helping situation and real life. He learns through new experience, through immediate experience, to will anew. He has met the outer reality, engaged with it, and moved into some fresh relation to it. And it is precisely because this same limitation is utterly natural to the helping situation, as it is to life itself, that the results can be what they are. Functional casework is sometimes accused of creating artificial limits or obstacles; sometimes students in the learning phase strive to create the limit in this same external or artificial way. But the progressive picture of the growth of skill has no such contrivance in it; if the helping process is real, the client searches for and finds the natural limits of the situation.

It is quite clear that this kind of choice does not take place in an intellectual process, or primarily through the exercise of reason which judiciously balances one alternative against another. The common view of the matter often maintains that emotion ought not to enter into the making of choices; that the choice is trustworthy only if it can be logically sustained by a literal weighing of values, by placing all the pros on one side of the scale and all the cons on the other, permitting whichever tilts heavier to determine the decision. Indeed, it is natural enough to draw this conclusion regarding the process of choice since, whenever the self is so engaged in choosing, it is true that its inner state seems to be describable as one in which the pros and cons thrash about, clash, separate, while one gains strength and another loses, until finally the moment can no longer be put off when the decision must be made and action taken.

The process of choice as we know it in helping bears no resemblance to a mechanical mental endeavor. The content of choosing carries and reflects the deeper psychological movement which is going on within the human self. In pure feeling, stripped of content, the experience of choice is an experience of the self in conflicted movement. The arresting fact is the seemingly nonintellectual nature of this movement at bottom, no matter what the justifications and rationalizations may be upon the surface. It is chaos, momentary or long lasting, consisting of clashes and divisions, unity and merging. It is fraught with discomfort, little discomforts in the form of irritation or big discomforts in the form of anguish and severing disunion. "At the instant of choice," says Kierkegaard, "he is in the most complete isolation, for he withdraws from his surroundings."[1]

It is the miraculous quality of living that some deep stream of the self flows along through time knowing its own direction for the sustenance of which it seems to select from its environment those bits of reality which carry this fundamental movement. At times the harmony of this inner direction is clear and unified. The self knows its way and chooses out of the common day rhythmically, with an organic sense of wholeness. At other times the disunity, the loss of relation, the loss of a focus for life itself seem to make of every tiniest commonplace decision an obstacle of wearying proportions. At times like these, even to decide what one wants to eat or what one should do next seems more than the available energy can cope with. It is then a blessed thing to have this question settled by another, without involvement of the self. In comparison, all love of freedom and all longing to "do it myself" fade into insignificance in the welcome relief of a situation or person which relieves the self of all responsibility.

Consequently, the helping person must also reckon with this powerful reverse of the desire to choose and to be independent. Even the best of helpers can be caught unwittingly in the temptation to project upon the other the pure, unadulterated supposition that the craving to be independent is the compelling factor. It is indeed a powerful craving, but it is just as true that there are times when the helping person knows, and is capable of utilizing fearlessly, the releasing, beneficent capacity of his own wholeness and strength to support momentarily the divided disunity of another.

It is the nature of this movement of the self in choice that it cannot happen at all except in time, and it is this which leads me to the conclusion, already put forth in the chapter on the client's initial movement toward the social agency, that the application process must contain at least three interviews, sufficiently spaced one from another so as to provide this essential time element in which reaction and development can take place. The three interviews constitute no arbitrary selection, since the accepted pattern of a completed process must allow for the beginning phase, the midpoint, and the ending phase. In the presence of the helper in the first interview, it is impossible for the applicant to discover, in all respects, what is himself and what is this powerful other with whom he has engaged. Neither can he discover this alone, but when he returns a second time he begins to work upon this question once more; he discovers that there are space and time in which to move around, and that allowance is made for the inevitable backward movement, which he must be able to admit and describe, if he is to be one who can utilize a continuing process.

Three interviews permit time, too, for the significant part played by the accidental intrusion of an external precipitant to take its course. The emphasis I have placed upon the deep stream of the self, which moves slowly and which carries the direction and purpose of the self, would not be complete without acknowledging at the same time the important and meaningful connection which exists between this fundamental self-direction and the accident of a chance happening or event. For example, when a student who has been in training for some time (and therefore has more capacity for accurate understanding of the experience) describes the series of events which brought him into training, he customarily describes a process long in the making, but very often a specific concrete event became the precipitant which moved him at last into action. We speak of this as the condition of "readiness" which develops in a long process of time, in which the external event finds fertile ground. This outer element is all-important in the process of choice, and the helping person, knowing this, can find ways to bring it into the process out of the natural happenings in the current situation.

The role of the helper in this process of enabling another to choose constructively might be said to consist of the capacity to relate simultaneously to this deepest level of the self, which carries the long slow direction, and to the surface level of the self, which carries the swift, more superficial levels of choice. Movement can perhaps be described as always having these two levels—at least two levels and seemingly at times many more. Knowing this, the helper accepts his unique role in this process in containing and holding the slower, more rhythmic movement while the client flounders around in indecision or premature decision, changes his mind a dozen times, tries out one thing, rejects another, and returns always to find the opportunity to reorganize his direction, until at last the precipitation of the ending creates the inescapable moment when he must take over into himself the responsibility for affirming, through word or action or both, that this is the way it will be.

This is the process of learning to choose, rich and comprised of plentiful activity. For choice cannot be made in a vacuum, nor can it be made in the head through thought alone. Choice becomes ever the more possible when there is content to be acted upon: things to do and problems to meet and solutions to try. Fear is easier to cope with when one can do something about the fear; sheer waiting and pondering are agony. Activity not only lends an outlet for the energy so stirred and aroused by the very helping situation itself, but it also plays that important role of facilitating discovery, through actual expression of the self, of what the self is like, and what it wants. It never ceases to fill me with wonder, each time I come upon the renewed recognition of how feeling changes through feeling: that is, through being expressed and lived out; how the will is better understood through willing and encountering the will of another; how every facet of experience, whether mistaken and painful or exhilarating and right, can be gathered into new comprehension by the self that is creatively focused, or, better said, in the moments when the self is creatively focused. When interviews are spaced at weekly intervals, as they very frequently are in the casework service, the hour of engagement between the helper and the one who seeks help can be intense, deeply disturbing, and penetrated by the new sense of life which every human being fears intensely yet craves so deeply. A week is none too long in which to thrash about in one's own aloneness—in confusion, in rebellion, in yielding, in conflict, all gathering toward the moment of return, in new organization, in new discovery of what the self is like by telling it to another whose responses are accurate. This is the part played by the focus: the penetration of the confusion, the break-up of the old constellation, as a result of which there ensues the giving way of the artificial defenses, and the mobilization of the self, made necessary by the very pressure of the next time now so imminent.

Sometimes it seems to happen that striking change in attitude and relationship comes about solely as the result of a client's yielding to emotion in relation to the helping person. Some casework material reflects this fact to a remarkable degree. What one sees in these circumstances is the initial tight organization of the client, coming forth in words and emotion that are hard, fixed, willful in the negative sense, destructive, and lacking in understanding of the part played by the own self. If and when a change of feeling does occur between the one seeking help and the helper when the emotion softens the will and true feeling bursts through, when the momentary relief from the tight organization is felt in this beneficent yielding to the emotion, then it is often highly possible that the fresh opening up of the capacity to feel love instead of hate makes itself manifest in every direction. Actually this has much that is characteristic of the growth process, and explains why so much helping appears to take place upon just this realization of unity with another. The helper who knows this organic wholeness can hold a total situation in momentary relief from disunity and separateness.

But no genuine growth will eventuate from this experience of unity alone. For now we come to the final piece which belongs in this consideration of the movement of the self in choice. If growth is in truth to be the outcome, then the final phase of the process requires of the one being helped that he take back into himself the will to do, and the belief that he has the strength to do; and, even more crucially, that he accept the final and ultimate outcome, that he must do it alone. This is the experience of separation, of utter aloneness, of final and inescapable responsibility. Throughout the helping process the helper has carried, in more or less degree, the will-to-growth, the identification with the potentiality of the client's self. At moments this is carried wholly by the helping person, but gradually, as the process develops, there are recurrent moments in which the client experiments with taking a piece of this other side back into some possessed and affirmed part of himself—all in gradual preparation for the terminating hour when the same thing must happen in final ending. He will try in every content that he knows to force the helping person to continue to carry this living side of himself, at the same time that the other movement in him is so powerful—the will to do it himself, to find the way himself, to possess and express his own, single, alone self. He will produce content to prove he has not been helped; he will reactivate all of his problem; he will seek to ensnare the helper in a new engagement of will. This is the reason why it is so valuable to set by agency structure the terminal point in the process, for it is only through long experience, and the finest of skill, that the helping person has what it takes to remain firm through all of this reactivation of problem, always produced no matter when the ending occurs. When time structure has been held to in this way, both helper and client know the inevitability of ending in this movement, with a deep feeling of satisfaction.

The one who has been helped has permitted himself to yield to another's whole; he has known vulnerability, incapable of defense when the core of the self is touched. He can leave the experience even though he desires to hold it, unique as it is in its quality of unity within a world where division is rampant. He will know the exhilarating, life-engendering sense of the strength now residing within his own self, where he finds the awareness of wholeness and unity heretofore sought for wholly outside. In this moment of time, where a true ending enables separation to be achieved and accepted, both helper and the one who has taken help know the truth which mankind denies—that freedom of choice can never be conferred as a gift from one to another, but must always be earned by the individual self.

NOTES

NOTE TO CHAPTER I

1. A recent publication undertakes to compare these differences, viz., *A Comparison of Diagnostic and Functional Casework Concepts*, Report of the Family Service Association of America Committee to Study Basic Concepts in Casework Practice, ed. Cora Kasius (New York: The Family Service Association of America, 1950).

NOTES TO CHAPTER II

1. The date 1880 is chosen because it appears to mark a significant turning point in the pre-casework period. Perhaps this is owing to the fact that the recorded history of social work year by year in the proceedings of national conferences begins at approximately this time.

2. The late Franklin K. Lane of California was Secretary of the Interior in the cabinet of President Wilson. He served from 1913 to 1920, retiring on March 1, 1920.

3. Mary E. Richmond, "Some Next Steps in Social Treatment," *Proceedings of the National Conference of Social Work*, 1920 (Chicago: University of Chicago Press, 1920), pp. 254-60.

4. *Ibid.*, p. 254.

5. *Ibid.*

6. Mary E. Richmond, *Friendly Visiting Among the Poor* (New York: The Macmillan Co., 1899).

7. The reader will note that the term "casework" is written in two different ways throughout these pages. This in itself is a change in custom reflected through language which, while apparently minor in importance, nevertheless reflects some change of a fundamental nature. Wherever quotations have been used from writing prior to 1930, the terms "social case work" or "case work" are consistently used. In my own writing I have maintained the accepted current use of the one word "casework."

8. George B. Buzelle, "Individuality in the Work of Charity," *Proceedings of the National Conference of Charities and Corrections*, 1886, ed. Isabel C. Barrows (Boston: Press of Geo. H. Ellis, 1886), pp, 185-88.

9. *Ibid.*, p. 187.

10. W. L. Bull, "Trampery: Its Causes, Present Aspects and Some Suggested Remedies," *Ibid.*, p. 188.

11. Alexander Johnson, "Preface," *Proceedings of the National Conference of Charities and Corrections*, at the Thirty-sixth Annual Ses-

sion held in the City of Buffalo, N. Y., June 9-16, 1909, ed. Alexander
Johnson (Fort Wayne: Press of Fort Wayne Printing Co., 1909), pp.
iii-iv.

12. Mary K. Simkovitch, "The Case Work Plane (or the Application
of the C.O.S. Method to Families above the Poverty Line)," *Ibid.*, pp.
136-49.

13. *Ibid.*

14. Mary E. Richmond, *Social Diagnosis* (New York: Russell Sage
Foundation, 1917).

15. See Virginia P. Robinson, *A Changing Psychology in Social Case
Work* (Chapel Hill: The University of North Carolina Press, 1930),
Part I. This book is only briefly referred to here, because in a later
chapter its influence upon developments in social work is more fully
examined.

NOTES TO CHAPTER III

1. Jessie Taft, "Progress in Social Case Work in Mental Hygiene,"
Proceedings of the National Conference of Social Work, 1923 (Chicago:
University of Chicago Press, 1923), p. 338.

2 Grace F. Marcus, "How Case-Work Training May Be Adapted to
Meet the Worker's Personal Problems," *Mental Hygiene*, XI (July,
1927), 455.

3. Jessie Taft, "The Function of a Mental Hygienist in a Children's
Agency," *Proceedings of the National Conference of Social Work, 1927*
(Chicago: University of Chicago Press, 1927), p. 392.

4. Jessie Taft, "Time as the Medium of the Helping Process," *Jewish
Social Service Quarterly*, XXVI (December, 1949), 189.

5. Jessie Taft, "The Function of a Mental Hygienist in a Children's
Agency," p. 396.

6. *Ibid.*, pp. 396, 398.

7. See the most recent statement of these developments, Virginia P.
Robinson, *The Dynamics of Supervision under Functional Controls*
(Philadelphia: University of Pennsylvania Press, 1949), Chap. II, pp.
16-26; also, Jessie Taft, "The Function of the Personality Course in the
Practice Unit," *Training for Skill in Social Case Work*, ed. Virginia P.
Robinson (Philadelphia: University of Pennsylvania Press, 1942), p. 62.

8. Virginia P. Robinson, *A Changing Psychology in Social Case Work*,
p. 127.

9. Jessie Taft, "Supervision of the Feeble-minded in the Community," *Proceedings of the National Conference of Social Work, 1918*
(Chicago: by the Conference, 1919), p. 548.

10. Jessie Taft, "Qualifications of the Psychiatric Social Worker,"
Proceedings of the National Conference of Social Work, 1919 (Chicago:
by the Conference, 1920).

11. See Jessie Taft, "Conception of the Growth Process Underlying
Social Casework Practice," *Social Casework*, XXXI (October, 1950), 311.

12. Virginia P. Robinson, "Organization of Field Work in a Professional School," *The Family*, I (October, 1920), 2.
13. *Ibid.*, p. 7.
14. Jessie Taft, "Problems of Social Case Work with Children," *Proceedings of the National Conference of Social Work*, 1920 (Chicago: University of Chicago Press, 1920), pp. 370-71.
15. *Ibid.*, p. 380.
16. Virginia P. Robinson, "Some Difficulties of Analyzing Social Interaction in the Interview," *Social Forces*, VI (June, 1928), 561.
17. Jessie Taft, "The Function of the Personality Course in the Practice Unit," *Training for Skill in Social Case Work*, p. 63.

NOTES TO CHAPTER IV

1. Virginia P. Robinson, *A Changing Psychology in Social Case Work*, p. xv.
2. Bertha Reynolds, "Review of A Changing Psychology in Social Case Work," *The Family*, XII (June, 1931), 111.
3. Virginia P. Robinson, "Psychoanalytic Contributions to Social Case-Work Treatment," *Mental Hygiene*, XV (July, 1931), 487-503.
4. Jessie Taft, "The Use of the Transfer within the Limits of the Office Interview," *The Family*, V (October, 1924), 143-46.
5. Virginia P. Robinson, *A Changing Psychology in Social Case Work*, p. 114.
6. Virginia P. Robinson, "Psychoanalytic Contributions to Social Case-Work Treatment," pp. 494-95.
7. Virginia P. Robinson, "A Discussion of Two Case Records Illustrating Personality Change," *Family Casework and Counseling, a Functional Approach*, ed. Jessie Taft (Philadelphia: University of Pennsylvania Press, 1948), p. 178.
8. The complete but concise statement of Dr. Taft's relation to psychotherapy, casework, and teaching, and its bearing upon the development of function, is to be found in a footnote in Chapter II, pp. 17-18, of Miss Robinson's most recent book, *The Dynamics of Supervision under Functional Controls*. The first part of this same chapter presents as well the most recent authoritative statement of Rank's relation to the development of the functional point of view.
9. Jessie Taft, *The Dynamics of Therapy in a Controlled Relationship* (New York: The Macmillan Co., 1937).
10. Jessie Taft (ed.), *The Relation of Function to Process in Social Case Work, Journal of Social Work Process*, Vol. I, No. 1, November, 1937 (Philadelphia: Pennsylvania School of Social Work, 1937).
11. Jessie Taft, "The Time Element in Therapy," *The American Journal of Orthopsychiatry* (January, 1933), pp. 65-79.
12. Otto Rank, *Will Therapy*, trans. Jessie Taft (New York: Alfred A. Knopf, 1936).

Notes

141

13. Otto Rank, *Truth and Reality*, trans. Jessie Taft (New York: Alfred A. Knopf, 1936).
14. Virginia P. Robinson, *Supervision in Social Case Work* (Chapel Hill: University of North Carolina Press, 1936).

NOTE TO CHAPTER VI

1. Rank, Otto, "Outline of a Genetic Psychology," p. 168. Unpublished material reproduced by the Pennsylvania School of Social Work from mimeographed notes of lectures which Dr. Rank released for use in the School.

NOTE TO CHAPTER VII

1. Virginia P. Robinson, "Some Difficulties of Analyzing Social Interaction in the Interview," p. 561.

NOTE TO CHAPTER VIII

1. Lawrence Pearsall Jacks, *Education Through Recreation* (New York: Harper & Bros., 1932), p. 41.

NOTES TO CHAPTER XII

1. Otto Rank, *Will Therapy*, trans. Jessie Taft (1 vol. ed.; New York: Alfred A. Knopf, 1945), p. 4.
2. *Ibid.*, p. 3.

NOTE TO CHAPTER XIII

1. Søren Kierkegaard, *Either/Or*, trans. Walter Lowrie (Princeton: Princeton University Press, 1944), II, 210.

www.ingramcontent.com/pod-product-compliance
Lightning Source LLC
Chambersburg PA
CBHW030653270326
41929CB00007B/340